Pete Bradshaw, author of *The Management of Self-Esteem* (Prentice-Hall/Spectrum Books, 1981), is founder and president of Organization Consultants, Inc., a Charlotte, North Carolina firm that provides counseling on personnel management and organization improvement. Mr. Bradshaw's clients include several of the top 50 American corporations, and a large number of smaller firms representing virtually every industry.

PETE BRADSHAW

Personal Power
How to build self-esteem and improve performance

Prentice-Hall, Inc., Englewood Cliffs, New Jersey 07632

A SPECTRUM BOOK

Library of Congress Cataloging in Publication Data
Bradshaw, Pete.
  Personal power.
  "A Spectrum Book."
  Bibliography: p.
  Includes index.
  1. Power (Social sciences) 2. Personality.
3. Self-respect. 4. Organizational behavior.
5. Performance. I. Title.
HM141.B826 1983   650.1   83-3043
ISBN 0-13-658153-6
ISBN 0-13-658146-3 (pbk.)

This book is available at a special discount when ordered in bulk quantities. Contact Prentice-Hall, Inc., General Publishing Division, Special Sales, Englewood Cliffs, N.J. 07632

© 1983 by Prentice-Hall, Inc., Englewood Cliffs, New Jersey 07632
All rights reserved. No part of this book may be reproduced in any form or by any means without permission in writing from the publisher.
A SPECTRUM BOOK. Printed in the United States of America.

1 2 3 4 5 6 7 8 9 10

ISBN 0-13-658153-6

ISBN 0-13-658146-3 (PBK.)

Editorial/production supervision by Alberta Boddy
Manufacturing buyer: Doreen Cavello
Cover design © 1983 by Jeannette Jacobs

Prentice-Hall International, Inc., *London*
Prentice-Hall of Australia Pty. Limited, *Sydney*
Prentice-Hall Canada Inc., *Toronto*
Prentice-Hall of India Private Limited, *New Delhi*
Prentice-Hall of Japan, Inc., *Tokyo*
Prentice-Hall of Southeast Asia Pte. Ltd., *Singapore*
Whitehall Books Limited, Wellington, *New Zealand*
Editora Prentice-Hall do Brasil Ltda., *Rio de Janeiro*

Contents

Preface *xi*

chapter one
Power *1*

chapter two
Self-esteem *5*

chapter three
Power and self-esteem *11*

chapter four
Power, fear, and guilt *23*

chapter five
**How we use
and project our power** *29*

chapter six
**The six power styles
and self-esteem** *43*

chapter seven
Overuse of one's power style *53*

chapter eight
Power and conflict *63*

chapter nine
**Some characteristics
of personal power
in organizations** *69*

chapter ten
**Organization assumptions
and personal power** *73*

chapter eleven
Some principles *83*

chapter twelve
Individuals as systems *89*

chapter thirteen
A case study *99*

chapter fourteen
Power and stress, *115*

chapter fifteen
Constraints and approaches to improving employee self-esteem *127*

chapter sixteen
What is power? *133*

Bibliography *137*

Index *141*

*This is for Holt and Elaine,
my children and also my friends.*

Preface

This is a book about the ways we use, abuse, and sometimes give away our ability to influence other people and events. It is about personal power and influence. It is also about the organizations and institutions through which power is expressed.

Power has been extensively examined in economic and political contexts, and the psychological need for power has been the subject of a considerable amount of research. In this post-Watergate, post-Vietnam era, power has also been exhaustively examined from governmental and societal perspectives. From biographies, autobiographies, and reports of investigative journalism we often get the flavor of the personal influence style wielded by this or that major figure. And several books describe techniques to demonstrate one's power in a variety of contexts.

All these varied sources are rich in ideas, insights, and detail, but they do not provide a systematic view of how power is expressed, why power is important, or how our individual uses of power and influence relate to other fundamental human desires.

Despite the attention given to power over the centuries, it has recently become somewhat fashionable to decry the use of power as somehow morally wrong or corrupt. As a nation, we have long distrusted institutionalized power. Indeed, the framers of our governmental structure established an elaborate system to prevent any one branch of government from becoming too dominant. Power is a fact of nature; it exists in the barnyard and the board room, the factory floor and the office. Power, like virtually every other human characteristic, can be used for good or ill.

Power is a little like fire, entirely real and exceedingly potent, yet probably very hard to describe to someone with no personal experience with it. Power, like fire, is by itself both neutral and undirected. It simply *is*. When controlled, fire can warm us, cook our food, and heat water to steam for driving mighty engines. Out of control, fire is a fearsome, all-consuming thing.

It is cold here and there is a log fire going in the fireplace. As the flames dance and jump, I am struck by how different every log fire is from every other log fire. Yet, every fire is like every other fire, too. All fires need oxygen and fuel and give off heat, light, and various gasses. Power is like that; it has endless variety and subtlety yet seems to obey some rules and have some common features. Power, like fire, is both a primitive force and a potential tool of enormous utility. In this book we will explore some of the characteristics and varieties of power and the ways we can and do direct this force to gain feelings of personal worth and value.

In *The Management of Self-Esteem* (Prentice-Hall, 1981) I describe a model or theory of self-esteem and the importance of personal power and influence to our sense of self-worth and value. Personal power and influence are primary sources of self-esteem. But power is more than that. The use of our personal power is the catalyst that permits self-respect to be gained from the other sources. The effective use of our personal influence is the instrument and the vehicle for gaining greater self-esteem from the other esteem sources and from the world around us.

We can readily observe how other people seem to use their power; on reflection, we can better understand what we do with our own. Probably most adults see and feel the varied uses of power most often in the educational, business, or governmental organization where so many of us earn our livelihoods. By organization, however, I mean any group of two or more people who regularly associate and who have some central reason to interact together. Business, family, governmental, fraternal, educational, religious, special interest, and other groups all fit this definition of organization. I do not mean to restrict the term *organization* to large groups such as massive corporations or governmental agencies; at the minimum, I mean any pair of people who see themselves as united in some significant way. This broad definition, therefore, includes couples and families.

This book is not a review of research evidence about power. David McClelland and others have amply demonstrated the existence of a need for power and have provided measurements of the need, but there has been little examination of the distinctive ways personal power may be used. Little has been written about how our individual use and projection of personal power relates to our overall feelings of worth and value, to our self-esteem. This book and the models described in it are more in the naturalistic than the empirical tradition. The main sources are my own and others' experiences and observations of how power is used in a range of organization settings and, to some extent, the behavior of historical figures.

I earn my living as a counsellor and advisor to organizations and to their managers and officials. My associates and I are regularly involved with a broad range of problems in an equally broad range of profit and not-for-profit organizations. Still, the majority of my experience is with business and industry. It is from this pragmatic perspective that we will consider self-esteem, power, and the ways they are expressed.

Personal power is one of the four sources of self-esteem. For that reason, Chapter 2 in this book briefly reviews the theory of self-esteem. Power plays a dual role: It is both a primary source of self-esteem and it is also the engine through which energy becomes invested in gaining self-esteem from all four sources. As an analogy, consider the person who is both player and coach of an athletic team. Power is like the player-coach— one of the team but also something more.

In this book we consider power largely from a personal, individual perspective and develop several models for observing and thinking about power in a more orderly way. Later in the book we examine some organizational consequences and implications. Personal power is the focus of this book; the organization is the main arena in which we will consider the effects of power.

To develop some ideas and models about personal power we have to consider the contexts in which power is used. For this reason, it will be worthwhile to examine organizations as systems and what they do to help or hinder the personal expression of one's power and influence. Throughout the book there are many examples; please consider an organization you know well and see how the ideas apply. There are several actual, although disguised, case studies for your consideration. The cases do not require any knowledge of the kind of company involved. The purpose is to help you see how the model of personal power applies. Additionally, there are several self-reflective exercises for your own use.

Any consideration of a subject like power requires choices and compromises, for power as a personal characteristic has enormous variety and color. Probably the major choice one faces in describing and analyzing power is the selection and elaboration, from great variety, of some set of coherent organizing categories and principles. We need some way to help make sense of power's complexity and to see its connection to other important aspects of our lives. If we draw out some patterns, it becomes much easier to think constructively about how we and others use power and how we might use it more productively.

The patterns, models, and principles described in this book have emerged from years of intensive work with a large number of supervisors, managers, and executives in a wide variety of organizations. In turn, the models have proven helpful to still more people in many situations.

A second choice in describing power is when to stop writing and allow the reader's own imagination, reflections, and observations to take over. A complete examination of power in all its theaters, forms, and applications would be truly encyclopedic and probably not very helpful to most people. On the whole, I have preferred to highlight what seem to be the most significant patterns and processes, described linkages to other important aspects of human behavior, tried to frame how power seems to work with a variety of examples, and provided some opportunity for additional reflections so that you can more easily connect the material to your own life.

There are many people who have contributed significantly to the ideas expressed here and to my own understanding and growth. My thanks go to Mack Livingston, Ed Pittman, and Sandra Shullman. But I owe most to Hugh Huntington, my friend and partner for many years. Once again, our lady about everything, Sue Funderburk, has my gratitude for preparing the manuscript and helping with the project in so many ways.

chapter one

Power

Have you ever left a discussion, confrontation, or other meeting and shortly thereafter suddenly felt you had been "had?" Did you feel angry or hurt? Did you find yourself mentally rehearsing what you might have said and done to meet some of your own wants and desires? Of course. You have probably experienced this feeling many times. Most of us have.

Whenever such a situation occurs, someone else has used his or her power to meet their individual desires at the expense of our own. Our negative feelings of decreased self-esteem show that we have *not* successfully used our own influence and power. The result is that we feel bad, or at the minimum less good, about ourselves as effective, competent people. We feel somehow diminished and discounted because our self-esteem has, in fact, been reduced.

Power is one of the four components of self-esteem. Evidence of personal power is important to each of us as a confirmation of the uniqueness and value of our individual self.

Our self-concept is the sum of who we know ourselves to be when we privately reflect on our behaviors, successes, failures, and strengths.

The way we feel about ourselves is directly influenced by the amount of power and influence we successfully exert over events and people. When we see that our behavior *causes* something to happen that we desire, or *causes* someone to act as we wish, we tend to feel good about who and what we are. Our self-esteem is increased. When we don't know *how* to have the influence we desire or when our efforts to exert power visibly fail, we feel diminished, frustrated, angry, or hurt. Sometimes we feel all of these.

The presence or absence of power has been a reality for all of us from before our earliest memories. That awareness may even have begun when we were summarily ejected from the warm, protected womb where our every need was automatically met. That sudden, unexpected expulsion into a sometimes harsh and uncaring world was, perhaps, our first experience with powerlessness. We didn't want it and we didn't cause it, but it happened anyway.

Since those first moments we have spent our lives trying with varying degrees of success to meet our desires, to bring about our wishes, and attempting to satisfy our individual wants and needs. That is what power ultimately is—the ability to bring about our desires.

With growth, experience, and change, each of us has learned a variety of ways of getting what we want. There is a rich diversity in the ways we individually express our power, a diversity that can continue to develop throughout our lives. The subtle expression of power to achieve our wants is very often what we really mean when we describe a person's style. It is even much of what we mean when we talk casually of someone's "personality." Think about someone you know reasonably well. Take a few moments to consider that person's style and the ways he or she relates to you. Using only behavior you have *recently* and *personally* seen, write a paragraph that describes that individual's approach. Save your description for use in Chapter Five.

Your behavioral description probably says something about how the person you selected influences people, situations, and events. This is natural because the ways we exercise our personal power to influence others are integral to our self-concept and are often visible to others.

The underlying forces, emotions and learnings that cause our behavior aren't visible. They can only be inferred. But the expression and use of power—the approaches and techniques we all use to get what we want—*are* visible. Our behavior, or what is actually done to meet some desire, can be seen. We can learn to recognize the preferred power behaviors of others and ourselves. We can learn to more deliberately select ways of expressing our power to increase the likelihood of meeting our desires.

When we are effective in using our own power to meet our wants we feel good about ourselves. We feel worthwhile, competent, and strong. Our self-esteem and self-respect are enhanced. When we are effective in using our power over some extended period of time, our overall self-concept becomes more positive. And with a more affirmative self-concept we become still more accomplished and skilled at exercising our power. The process resembles an upward spiral.

The reverse is also true. Many people feel themselves to be largely without influence. They are unsure how to use their power. Perhaps they don't know how to use their influence, or they feel the use of power is somehow wrong or immoral. Others may repeatedly find themselves the unwilling recipients or targets of the power behaviors of another. When that happens to us, we will probably feel manipulated. When we do what others desire at the expense of our own wants, needs, or beliefs, we become aware of powerfully negative feelings. We might, for example, feel weak and discounted as a worthwhile human being. We can feel hurt, frustrated, sad, and angry.

One of the most common, though rarely acknowledged, reasons for severing personal and organization relationships is one's perception that he or she is essentially without power and influence to meet his or her wants in the relationship. Employee turnover, the breakdown of friendships, absenteeism, and divorce are all consequences of self-esteem being unbearably reduced in a particular relationship. Often the erosion in self-respect results from feeling powerless and essentially helpless to meet our wants and needs. Feelings of anger and sadness are common symptoms of this process.

The central importance of the need for personal power can also be seen in supposedly rational, unemotional, and hardheaded business activities like the decision to merge business organizations. Both our own consulting experience and the research of others suggest that the enhancement of personal power, and perhaps prestige, is frequently the real impetus behind such decisions by corporate officers. The resistance of top executives to merger or acquisition overtures may also reflect more a personal desire to retain power than purely rational business motives.

This is not to say the desire for personal power and influence is in some way bad. It is to say the motivation to preserve and enhance personal power is often a crucial element in many of our individual choices and decisions.

chapter two

Self-esteem

I believe there is a basic, powerful need in nearly all of us to feel that we are unique, effective, and worthwhile. We need to be able to generally approve of ourselves. When we feel good about ourselves, our behavior is characterized by openness, experimentation, a willingness to expose ourselves, and a commitment to our goals. Not surprisingly, under such conditions we will tend to be quite effective in important areas of our lives.

The reverse is also true; when we do not feel fundamentally good about ourselves, our effectiveness will usually be reduced in one or another major areas of our lives. We will often act and feel depressed, lethargic, uninvolved, unresponsive, and closed to experience and growth. A positive sense of self-esteem and self-respect is critical to most of us. It was critical in our formative years in the development of our sense of self and who we are. It is critical now as we interact with the world around us. Power is a major source of self-esteem. Because it plays a key, catalytic role in our ability to gain self-esteem from all sources, we must briefly examine the theory of self-esteem. In this way we can better understand the importance and uses of power to our sense of self-worth and value.

There seem to be four sources of self-esteem:

1. Evidence of increasing personal power, control, and influence over events significant to us as unique individuals. In a business, financial approval authority may be of minimal importance to some of us, but to others it may be important as an indicator of power and influence.

2. Visible achievement and accomplishment of goals and objectives, particularly goals we have established for ourselves. These can be relatively trivial goals to an outside observer, but important to us from a personal, self-esteem perspective.

3. A clear sense of being valued and cared about as a worthwhile human being. Evidence of compassion from others, or having someone personally important to us listen and care about us are examples. Relationships characterized by trust and the open sharing of sensitive feelings is another example.

4. Opportunities and permission to behave in ways congruent with deeply held value and belief systems. Honesty in dealing with customers, if that is a deeply valued behavior, would be esteem-enhancing. But if less than honest behaviors were required or rewarded by the organization, the conflict with one's own values might well reduce one's self-esteem.

Figure 2.1 shows one way to visualize self-esteem, its four components, and our self-concept. This hydraulic model suggests that for each of us there is a pool of possible self-esteem enhancing conditions and situations.

Self-esteem is at least potentially available from any or all of these sources. The sum of input from all four sources is the self-esteem income we experience as feeling basically good or bad about ourselves and our lives. The self-concept is the private picture we have of who and what we are. It consists of memories of experiences we had as children and as adults either gaining or losing self-esteem. The self-concept is a recording of the feelings of our successes and failures in gaining self-esteem from one or more of the four sources.

But for most of us, our self-concept is not frozen in past experience. Our ideas about who we are, our strengths, and our weaknesses can and do change with experience. For example, as youngsters we may have had only failure in trying to achieve athletic prowess. If such skill was especially important to us and highly valued by important people in our small

Our Life Space   **Our Bucket**

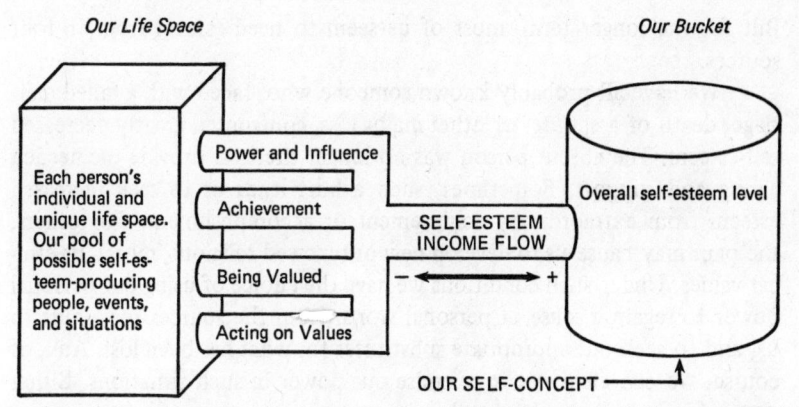

FIGURE 2.1. (From *The Management of Self-Esteem*, by Pete Bradshaw. © 1981 by Prentice-Hall, Inc., Englewood Cliffs, New Jersey 07632.)

world, we may have had little esteem income from achievement. Later, perhaps we found that school work presented an arena in which we could excel. If that expression of achievement was important and valued, then we may at last have gained significant self-esteem from accomplishment and achievement. With growth, experience, and change in our self-esteem income, our self-concept also continues to change.

The theory of self-esteem includes both past and present factors in our lives. The model shows the potential available to all of us for increased self-esteem. When we obtain adequate self-esteem from the four sources, we feel alive. Our world is generally bright and exciting, full of challenge and opportunity. When we feel fundamentally good about who and what we are as a unique, intrinsically worthwhile person, we tend to be expressive, risk-taking, creative, and open to experience. These are some of the benefits of a high level of self-esteem.

But when we have a low level of esteem income from one or more of the four sources, the reverse tends to be true. We see ourselves as not very effective and not very worthwhile. This is a painful and searing thing. Under such conditions we tend to be withdrawn, overly cautious, routine in our actions, and insensitive or defensive about new experiences.

It seems that most people can compensate for low esteem income from any one of the four sources. We seem to do this by redoubling our efforts to gain positive feelings about ourselves from the remaining sources.

But for the longer term, most of us seem to need esteem from all four sources.

We have all probably known someone who, faced with a failed marriage, death of a spouse, or other major loss, confronted greatly decreased self-esteem. The absent person was no longer there to provide the needed caring and support. Sometimes, such a hurt leads us to seek increased esteem from extraordinary achievement or accomplishment. For others, the pain may cause us to develop new or renewed religious, moral, or ethical values. Under such conditions we have the choice of using our personal power to regain a sense of personal worth from the sources remaining to us, and to seek out appropriate substitutes for what has been lost. And, of course, we can elect not to exercise our power in such situations. Either choice has major behavioral and emotional consequences.

One of the major ways we can deliberately increase our self-esteem is by learning to better project and apply our power and influence. Through understanding, reflection, and rehearsal we can learn to select ways to more effectively use our influence. We can develop awareness of the uses of power by others and increase our own power skills. When we become more accomplished at using power, we meet more of our needs and desires from all available sources of esteem. This highlights the dual nature of power. It is both a source of self-esteem and an energizer that enables esteem to be gained from all sources. It is analogous to a pump for the hydraulic system in Figure 2.1.

Our awareness of the power behaviors of others and our own preferred uses of power develop with experience, perhaps beginning with birth. As young children, some of us had essentially positive experiences in projecting our power and were largely able to have many of our desires met. Others may have been less successful and found themselves often without much influence in meeting their wants. Those early experiences of successfully or unsuccessfully projecting our own power had an enormous impact on our sense of who and what we are, even as young children. It is true, though, that we are not captives of the past. We can deliberately choose to increasingly use our own influence and power. In doing so, we can modify our self-concept. We are a mixture of then and now. Both influence our sense of who we are and how we feel about ourselves. The impact of past and present events on the early self-concept, on the present level of self-esteem and on our developing self-concept are shown in Figure 2.2.

FIGURE 2.2. (From *The Management of Self-Esteem*, by Pete Bradshaw. © 1981 by Prentice-Hall, Inc., Englewood Cliffs, New Jersey 07632.)

Early Self-Concept and Preferred Sources of Self-Esteem

SOURCES OF PRESENT SELF-ESTEEM
(Positive or Negative)
- Relationships
  Family, friends, supervisor, co-workers, and subordinates.
- Non-work activities
  Hobbies, continuing education, civic, church, social, and home.
- Work-related activities
  Interest, challenge, visible achievement, advancement, rewards, freedom-of-action, access to information, inclusion, involvement, influence, relationships, power, being valued, compassion, and future potentials.

X =

PRESENT LEVEL OF SELF-ESTEEM INCOME

PRESENT SELF-CONCEPT

COMPONENTS AND SOURCES OF EARLY SELF-ESTEEM
- Successes and achievements, growth of skill, and efficacy; failures of accomplishment and result.
- Experiences with being cared for, valued, and accepted as worthwhile; experiences with being rejected, discounted, and ignored.
- Demonstrating personal influence and power over events and other people, demonstrating powerlessness, low influence, and being manipulated.
- Development of basic belief and value system and adherence to such a system; lack of development of such a system or inability to act congruently with such beliefs and values.

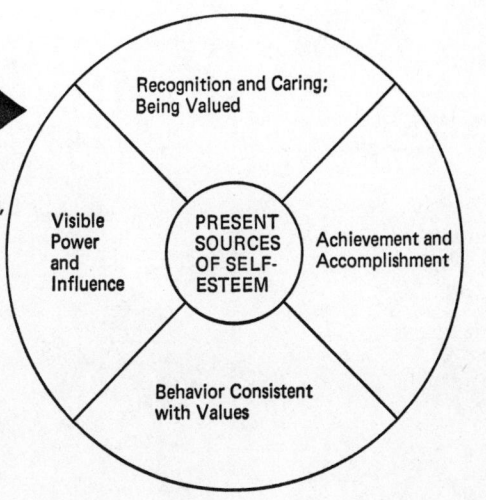

PRESENT SOURCES OF SELF-ESTEEM
- Recognition and Caring; Being Valued
- Achievement and Accomplishment
- Behavior Consistent with Values
- Visible Power and Influence

Figure 2.2 shows the sources of early self-esteem arising from successes or failures in each of the four primary areas. The result of these successes and failures was our early idea of who we were—our identity and early self-concept. Because in the past we were successful in gaining positive feelings about ourselves from one or another of the four sources, many of us even now tend to return to that source and to repeat those successful behaviors. We have developed one or more preferred sources of self-esteem.

But for most of us growth didn't automatically cease at some point in the past. Nor did our need for self-esteem. Relationships, work, and non-work activities are some potential avenues for self-esteem right now. We can consider various life situations as self-esteem income possibilities. The four sources or components of self-esteem we have discussed help us order and organize the bewildering array of esteem-producing possibilities.

Our early self concept together with increases or decreases in esteem in the present combine to yield our present sense of satisfaction or dissatisfaction with who we are. Over time, our self-concept can change, sometimes minimally and sometimes markedly. We have only modest opportunities to do much about our early self-concept. We have enormous possibilities for enhancing our present self-esteem and ultimately influencing our self-concept.

The factor that permits us to realize some of these possibilities for growth and change is the effective expression of our personal power.

chapter three

Power and self-esteem

Power and its expression are critical to a positive sense of self-worth. The expression and use of our personal power and influence ultimately permits us to gain self-esteem from all four sources. The desire for power and influence is the energizer, the impetus, and the drive that impels us to action. It is through such action that self-esteem becomes more available from all four categories. Through the use of our personal power we can create self-esteem income for ourselves.

For example, suppose there is little visible evidence of achievement or accomplishment in your work. You can see few measurable results, progress toward your goals is not clear, and there is little feedback about your effectiveness from your supervisor. Under such conditions, your self-esteem may be reduced so that it can be real drudgery just to go to work. Many people just go along with such a situation feeling progressively less productive and increasingly bored. This condition saps energy and drains commitment. But other people will, even at some risk, use their power to cause change.

Some will request and even demand that their supervisors give them periodic performance reviews. Others will establish goals and performance standards of their own. Still others will quietly begin to investigate other employment possibilities. They may do so even to the extent of changing the nature and direction of their careers. I know several senior level, large company managers who became so frustrated by their inability to accomplish anything that they sought out and now happily occupy positions where their personal contributions are clear. One has become a skilled carpenter and makes fine furniture. Another purchased a failing country store and has successfully applied his considerable talents to improving the store's profitability.

Both of these people used their power to try to change conditions within their previous organizations. Both failed to cause enough change to give them adequate self-esteem from accomplishment and achievement. Their use of their power was not successful. And, in very different ways, each then used his power to create conditions where evidence of personal impact and achievement is now clear and highly visible. The projection of one's power sometimes carries risk—both of these executives initially failed. But through the expression of their individual power, each later succeeded. Power is the force that can permit self-esteem to be gained from the world around us.

A manager of a large plant gradually became much more aware and disapproving of the industrial pollution caused by his operation. He developed a strong value for relatively nonpolluted air and water, like many managers in his position over the past twenty years or so. This manager found himself in a particularly severe conflict. His plant (an iron foundry), was a major polluter of a nearby river and the surrounding air. For him, it was a moral and ethical issue.

His immediate superiors would not or felt they could not provide the funds necessary for anti-pollution equipment needed to eliminate the problem. In a series of progressively higher level meetings, the plant manager stated his case: Such pollution could be largely eliminated, and the company's good profits made the equipment affordable. Moreover, to knowingly permit the continuing pollution was both morally and legally wrong in his view.

The conflict in values was beginning to cause this manager, with a fine record and excellent prospects, to seriously consider resigning. He told me at the time:

> Hell, I just don't like myself very much. It is just plain wrong to do what we're doing, and I'm in charge. I can't go on this way.

His initial efforts involved attempting to establish a new plant budget category for the necessary equipment. That line of the proposed budget was deleted by his superiors as an unnecessary expense. His next attempt to influence the company's actions was the preparation of a detailed study and the projection of costs, schedules, and benefits. All available and appropriate equipment was considered by the plant's engineers, and tentative equipment selections were made.

That effort also failed. The plant manager's superior responded with:

> Look, Harold, I know you feel strongly about this. But harping on it isn't going to help your career. We'll get to it (fixing the problems) but I don't want to hear anything more about it. Just leave your study with me.

At this point, the manager was depressed, frustrated and confused. He seemed unable to have any influence on solving a major personal conflict in values. He continued for a time to operate the plant as usual. By doing so, he continued to act directly counter to his strong belief. As we have seen, he felt progressively worse about himself and seriously considered leaving the company. A deliberate choice to leave would, indeed, have been an expression of personal power. But for this manager, leaving was the final option. It was not one he wanted to exercise because he felt loyal to the company and a genuine affection for the president and some of the other senior executives who had guided his career.

He determined to try to influence the situation by directly confronting his superiors and, if necessary, escalating the problem to the president. The norms governing managerial behavior in this firm were, as in so many others, that a subordinate virtually never bypassed his superior to gain approval for a rejected plan or proposal. Conventional wisdom in that organization was that to bypass one's boss was a guarantee of a foreshortened career or, at the minimum, an extended stagnant and unpleasant period.

In a difficult and emotional confrontation with his superiors, this manager stated his intention to take the issue directly to the president, and he invited his superiors to participate in the meeting with the president. Only then did it become clear that his superiors had never brought the subject up with the president or any other senior official. The power projected by the plant manager broke the logjam. His superiors did attend the meeting and, interestingly, supported his position. In a matter of weeks, funds had been allocated and work had started to correct the various problems.

The deliberate use of one's personal power and influence is often necessary if we are to obtain self-esteem from the remaining three sources. But by itself, the successful projection of one's power provides self-esteem and a sense of personal worth and value. Shortly after the episode, I asked the plant manager to describe his feelings:

> It was one of the hardest things I've ever done, and probably the most worthwhile. It fixed something (the polluting conditions) that was terribly wrong any way you look at it. And that feels just great. The company and I are back in synch. I'm proud of the company.
>
> Also, by really using my force and determination in a straight-up way, I got something done that didn't succeed at all when I tried other, easier approaches like the studies and informational presentation.
>
> But, I'll tell you something. It felt damn good to impose my wants and to get that son of a bitch going *my* way.

Power, then, is the driving force often needed for us to gain self-esteem from the other sources. And it is also true that the application of one's influence is, by itself, self-esteem producing.

During the last ten years or so citizen action groups have emerged as a powerful force in many cities and towns. An examination of a variety of such groups and their histories shows an increasingly sophisticated use of power. Most such groups seem to have coalesced around a limited and specific issue. More often than not the driving emotion was anger over the action or inaction of some governmental unit. It was often not college aged rebels, minority people, or poor people who started such grass roots efforts. Rather it was often relatively affluent middle class people in the mainstream of their communities.

The earliest stage for many of these groups seems to have been marked by informal meetings among concerned and vocal individuals who may or may not have had previous contact. The next phase was typically vociferous, characterized by demonstrations, marches, and sometimes vandalism and violence. This represented a noisy but generally unsophisticated and ineffective use of power. To be sure, the group often attracted the attention of those it opposed and the public, but was also frequently dismissed as unimportant and impotent. During this phase, power and influence were diffuse, undirected, and often squandered.

Ultimately successful groups seem to have next entered a stage where one or more typically independent, persuasive, and charismatic leaders emerged, took control, and were, sometimes grudgingly, accepted by the group. At this point, power began to be applied in increasingly targeted and sophisticated ways. Such groups and their leaders often became adept at using the media. They could and did turn out blocks of voters for or against a variety of candidates and issues. They became accomplished fund-raisers, and launched a large number of creative legal challenges.

Many of these citizen groups today are recognized power blocs. In many cases, they are institutions in their own right. Generally, too, a different type of leader from the charismatically independent person now directs the organization. An ability to negotiate, to create a broad-based consensus for action, and a deliberate involvement of a range of personalities, skills, and backgrounds seem to mark the new leaders. The history of many such citizen action groups can be described in terms of the way power was used to gain influence. Successful groups seem, somehow, to have been led by people with a personal approach to power appropriate to the group and time. While power is expressed through organizations, it is ultimately a personal, human characteristic not, as such, a characteristic of groups or organizations.

The use of personal power to gain self-esteem is not limited to a particular economic objective in a setting such as business, industry, or an interest group. For example, increasing numbers of women are entering the business world. Recurring economic uncertainties and inflation may produce the need for a second income, but many women are entering or reentering the workplace for reasons quite different from a purely economic motive.

Perhaps a woman married expecting her life to be fulfilled by caring for her husband, by bearing and raising children, by creating a comfortable home, and, possibly, becoming involved in a favorite hobby such as painting or gardening. She may have contemplated contributing time and effort to some charitable or community-oriented projects.

As the years pass, her husband becomes ever more concerned with his work. The children grow and become increasingly less dependent as they develop their own interests and abilities to cope. The home is established, and the charitable or civic involvements now seem tedious, repetitive, or boring.

Is it any wonder that so many women in such situations describe themselves as depressed, sad, or anxious? The reason for such powerful feelings is a steady, almost imperceptible, loss of self-esteem from one or more of the four sources. There may be little opportunity for visible achievement or accomplishment for such a woman. The children and husband are gone to work or school most of the day. There are only so many curtains to make or walls to paint. So her self-esteem suffers because she can see few opportunities for real accomplishment.

Moreover, the expression of love and caring often becomes less and less frequent in a marriage of many years. The children, too, develop other attachments and interests. We should not be surprised, then, at the results of some recent polls that suggest that as many as forty-five or fifty percent of married women say they have been involved in at least one extramarital relationship. I'm aware of no quantitative data, but suspect the percentage of men who have been so involved would be similar.

In a world bounded by an often empty home, a husband immersed in "making it" in his profession or career, and opportunities for personal influence limited to offering advice about country club or charitable organization matters, many women feel powerless. They, in fact, have few opportunities for the expression of their personal power and influence. The result is a predictable reduction in self-esteem.

In three of the four areas we have considered as essential components of self-esteem, such a woman suffers. Predictably, she will not feel good about herself, and may feel depressed, sad, or angry. She might try to dampen the pain with a variety of sexual partners, with drugs, or with alcohol. Or she may choose to use her personal power to change the boundaries of her world so that esteem becomes more available. The exercise and projection of her personal power in making the change will *itself* help to significantly increase her sense of personal worth and value.

To the extent that she locates or creates a situation where visible achievements, satisfying relationships, and opportunities to have some influence are available, her self-esteem will improve. But the key element is the initial choice to exercise personal power to change a dissatisfying situation. Increasing numbers of women are now doing just that. They are entering or reentering business, opening shops, returning to school to gain marketable skills, and running for political office.

The projection of personal power carries risk. The plant manager we met earlier clearly risked a promising career. The woman who asserts her independence of husband and home may risk unhappiness in her marriage, or even divorce. But the alternative to the projection of one's personal power and influence is a steady decline in one's feelings of personal worth, value, and effectiveness. With such a reduction in self-esteem come powerful feelings of anger, sadness, fear, depression, and even grief.

For many people in recent years employment opportunities have become increasingly bleak in the cities and towns where they have spent their lives. Many previously healthy industries have failed, moved, or greatly reduced their levels of employment. Governmental unemployment benefits, employer-granted severance pay, and union funds have all been depleted, and in many cases exhausted. The raw numbers and statistics are grim enough. But what of the individual employee who is often loyal, competent, and has many years of service to a particular employer?

For the most part, laid-off employees are totally powerless to influence the economic events that led to the reductions in staff. When entire industries are damaged, employees often find it impossible to transfer their specialized skills to any other employer, which is another example of their powerlessness. Many have family ties and unsaleable homes that limit new job opportunities. The satisfaction of having given a good day's work for a good day's pay is gone. No longer can these employees see the results of their work in a paycheck or in visible accomplishments and achievements in the form of useful products and services or satisfied customers.

For many, strong family and friendship ties are the only source of self-esteem left. But esteem from this source can also be reduced because close work relationships are fractured by the layoff.

Under these conditions some will turn to religious values and beliefs for a renewed sense of self-worth and value. For those who previously worked for large, stable, and dependable companies, decades-old beliefs in the ultimate security of such organizations has been irreparably shattered. And many union members now question the philosophy of holding out for every possible gain at the bargaining table regardless of consequences. Many long-time beliefs, then, may seem much less dependable. Some will move to another city or region, others will seek to gain new and different skills, and others may develop an avocation or hobby into a full-time occupation. All of these are ways of using power. Others, however, may simply withdraw and feel increasingly depressed and worthless as their self-esteem drains away.

Each of us must decide whether and when the rewards of increased self-esteem and the associated feelings of aliveness, creativity, optimism, and joy are worth the risk. It is our choice to make. Let me share a personal example. As consultants, we often perform work at several business locations of a particular client company. Sometimes, after a series of such engagements, patterns of executive or organization behavior emerge that impact the performance of a number of locations. When this happens, we will seek to meet with senior corporate executives to summarize what seem to be issues common and important to the several locations and to present our suggestions and recommendations. These sessions nearly always involve vigorous give and take. There is a probing of our reasoning and a mutual, creative exploration of alternatives. Such meetings are, almost without exception, challenging and energizing for consultants and client executives alike. My associates and I usually leave with a sense of satisfaction, effectiveness, and fulfillment. Many client executives have told us that they, too, have these positive feelings. Most of those involved, then, are left feeling good about themselves. We experience a positive sense of personal value and efficiency, of self-esteem.

The process permits and encourages everyone to have significant influence on the design and conduct of future activities. Everyone can see some achievement and accomplishment as results are shared, plans laid, and resources selected and committed. We develop a warm feeling of comraderie, of sharing and caring as difficult issues are directly confronted, and better levels of understanding and trust are reached.

It is not uncommon in these sessions (sometimes there may be a series) for ethical issues and value questions to arise. Typically, such questions concern the proper treatment of people at various levels, but sometimes issues of equal opportunity, product quality, or environmental effects are involved. Once again, we have usually found great sensitivity to such matters on the part of top level executives, despite the frequent but inaccurate characterization of business leaders as uncaring, unaware, and insensitive. The very process of bringing such issues to the surface, confronting and at least attempting to solve them increases the self-esteem of participants. Many of those involved have told us of feeling very good about helping to create an organization policy more consistent with their own personal values.

In one recent, unusual situation, we met with a senior executive and several of his subordinates to review and summarize our findings, predictions, and suggestions. But he refused to become involved. He asked virtually no questions, surfaced no disagreements, and, in general, was only marginally involved. He simply seemed withdrawn and disinterested, despite our many efforts to arouse his interest. When several clearly illegal and unethical situations in one location were described, he showed no interest or concern. At long last we directly confronted our own frustration. We stated that the process was proving to be very dissatisfying to us and asked the executive, "How well is this process meeting your needs? Are you gaining what you wish from this meeting?"

After a pause, he said, "No. When are we going to get to the specific answer?" Even his subordinates were taken back. They, too, felt several very specific alternatives had been considered, although without the executive's real involvement.

There are at least two key processes that characterize effective communication. First there must be relatively candid exposure of the views, ideas, facts, and feelings possessed by each party. Second, there must be feedback from each party about his or her facts, opinions, and concerns. Both of these can, and ideally should, be active processes. I can choose to reveal my ideas, facts, and feelings to you or withhold them. And I can choose to seek out your facts, feelings and ideas—or not. Both processes involve the use of one's power and influence.

In the case of the reticent executive, mutual exploration simply didn't happen. Despite our best efforts, we could not influence that executive's behavior, and we could not obtain his concerns, knowledge, or ideas. We sought feedback from him, but were unable to gain very much. Those in the meeting were essentially powerless. We had little influence, and could gain no appreciable sense of accomplishment and achievement. The usual glow and accompanying pleasant feelings of group cohesiveness were lacking after the meeting.

As we tried to analyze what had happened, I realized that my own feelings were a mixture of anger and sorrow. When I asked several other participants how they felt, they used these words:

Depressed	Sad
Sour	Drained
Empty	Mad
Angry	Manipulated
Frustrated	Dissatisfied

These feelings are usually accurate indicators of low self-esteem.

When we compare these kinds of feelings with those that arise from the more typical exploration sessions described earlier, the difference is clear. In this particular session, the feelings of personal worth and value usually evident were not realized.

1. Participants were powerless and largely without influence.
2. There was little evidence of accomplishment and achievement.
3. Few if any participants felt valued and cared-about.
4. Participants were aware of some significantly negative ethical and legal issues, but those issues were not resolved. Thus, a conflict existed for some between their values and those apparently tolerated by senior management.

As advisors, we were *willing* to use our personal power to change the nature of the meeting, but we were not *successful* in doing so. That is why my associate and I felt less negative about ourselves than did the other participants. We *did* confront the issue and attempt to change the nature of the meeting. Some other participants who were equally dissatisfied chose not to be confrontive. They deliberately elected to give their power away. And as several later told us, they felt badly about themselves as a result.

> Hell, it was awful. I just sat there. I should have said, "Look, Charlie (the senior executive present), we're not getting anywhere. You have to be involved. What do you *want* from us, or from Pete and Hugh?"

When you leave a meeting and overhear statements like, "I should have said . . . ", or "What was that all about?" you can bet that some key issues were not confronted and that the self-esteem of at least some participants has been decreased. You can also bet that power was given away by most of those who are not satisfied.

Deliberately choosing to use one's personal power to cause change and to meet one's needs is not always going to succeed. But even when such efforts do not succeed in obtaining esteem from the other sources, there *is* a sense of self-worth and personal value in having tried.

EXERCISE: THE POWER OF OTHERS

Think about your experiences at work, with your parents, your spouse, with salespeople, your boss, or others.

1. Have you ever felt pressured to do something you really did not want to do? When? By whom? What did you do? How did you use your own power?

2. Did you ever feel you *had* to agree to some plan or action against your own judgment? What was it?
3. Were you ever pressured or persuaded to do something or agree to something that somehow felt wrong or inadvisable?
4. When you felt manipulated or forced, and all of us have, how did *you feel*? Depressed? Angry? Confused? Sad? Enraged? These are common reactions to being coerced, however subtly, by others.

Write a description of the event(s) (there may be several). Then think of how someone used their power, and you did not. Be as ruthlessly candid as you can in reflecting on the questions above. Who did what? To whom? When? And with what effect? Consider that the effect is *not* just some agreement. It *is* how you felt. What did *you* learn by examining the effectiveness of your personal power and influence style?

There is space provided below for you to write your answers to the questions.

1. _____

2. _____

3. _____

4. _____

chapter four

Power, fear, and guilt

This book is about power and influence. Not only is personal power itself a major potential source of self-esteem and of positive feelings about ourselves, but it is also the means by which we can gain access to greater self-esteem from all four sources. Figure 4.1 shows this process.

For example, we can deliberately use our own power to create or seek out situations at work or elsewhere to gain greater opportunity for visible achievement. We can decide to improve our competence and knowledge through study and other educational experiences. In doing so, we improve our chances to feel the joy of achievement in some area. We might elect to seek out a new position, a new employer, or even an entirely different line of work where our achievements and accomplishments are more clearly the visible result of our personal effort and skill. Or, of course, we can simply wait in hopes that things will somehow improve.

Or, if our esteem income from being valued and cared about is not adequate, we can choose to use our own power to find ways to broaden our social contacts. We might deliberately seek out and reestablish ties with old friends or try to rejuvenate a tired marriage. Some of us might try to make real contact with our children, perhaps for the first time. But

FIGURE 4.1. The Self-Esteem Process. (From *The Management of Self-Esteem*, by Pete Bradshaw. © 1981 by Prentice-Hall, Inc., Englewood Cliffs, New Jersey 07632.)

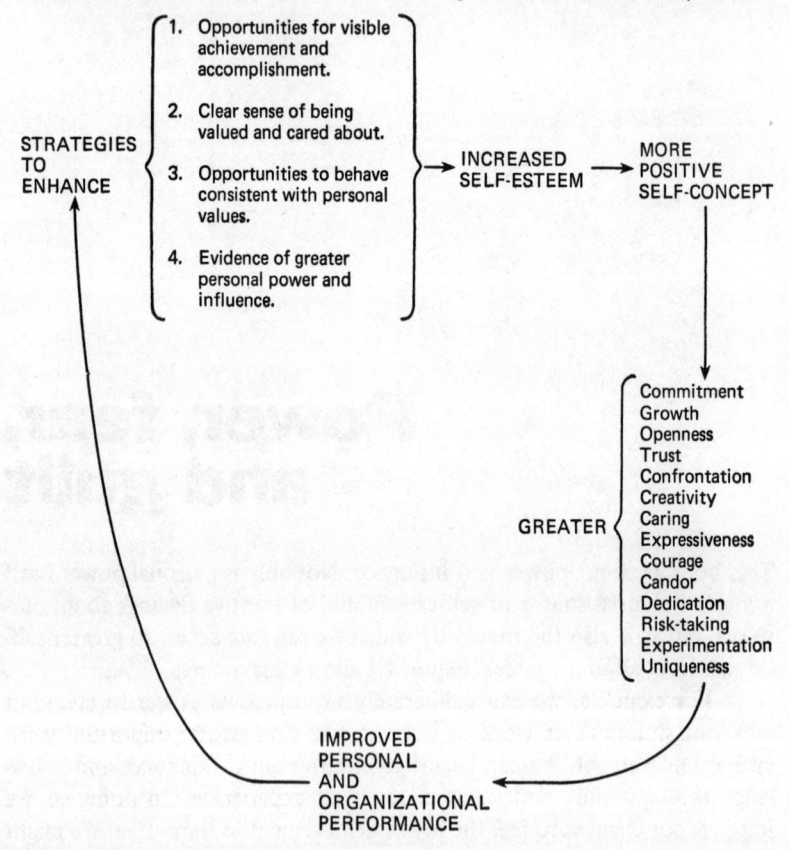

STRATEGIES TO ENHANCE
1. Opportunities for visible achievement and accomplishment.
2. Clear sense of being valued and cared about.
3. Opportunities to behave consistent with personal values.
4. Evidence of greater personal power and influence.

→ INCREASED SELF-ESTEEM → MORE POSITIVE SELF-CONCEPT

GREATER
Commitment
Growth
Openness
Trust
Confrontation
Creativity
Caring
Expressiveness
Courage
Candor
Dedication
Risk-taking
Experimentation
Uniqueness

IMPROVED PERSONAL AND ORGANIZATIONAL PERFORMANCE

others of us will allow ourselves to suffer the pain of loneliness and feelings of isolation without using our power to change, improve or develop potentially caring relationships.

Many people find themselves in positions where they feel compelled to behave in ways counter to deeply held values and beliefs. But are we really *forced* to act in opposition to our values? Or, do we *choose* not to change the contradictory situation and our place in it? Managers and supervisors have often told me of being *forced* by higher authority to take personnel actions, such as employee layoffs or dismissals, when the required action was in their view morally and ethically wrong. People often stay in marriages knowing that their partner no longer cares for them and is emotionally and physically involved with another person. For some, this situation presents a major moral and ethical dilemma. Once again, some of us will simply go along with the demands or with the situation while others will elect to use their personal power to cause change.

If we deliberately choose to project our personal power and influence, our self-esteem is enhanced. When we use our power to change those situations so that the remaining three sources are once again contributing feelings of self-worth, we increase our self-esteem from one or more of the other sources as well. Our own power and influence, when used to gain self-esteem, is a multiplier in its effect on our feelings and emotions.

Power has most often been considered in either social or political contexts. This book is about *personal* power. Personal power is:

> One's effort to deliberately modify significant aspects of one's environment (personal, social, physical or professional) to increase one's sense of self-worth and value.

Our sense of worthiness—our self-esteem—is directly related to the deliberate and effective use of our personal influence and power. Indeed, significant levels of self-esteem over a long period of time do not seem possible in the absence of successful use of personal power.

There are two critical issues embedded in the above statement: Our *willingness* to use our power and our *success* in doing so. Many people avoid using their own influence and power even when they would probably succeed. Others of us are more likely to try to influence some portion of our environment even though we sometimes fail. Obviously, we cannot succeed in enhancing our self-esteem if we deny or avoid using our power. Why, then, do so many of us avoid using our power to try to make the changes needed for us to feel good about who we are as unique, worthwhile people? In a word, fear.

Modern man has evolved from more primitive creatures. Our ancestors crouched around the fire at the cave's mouth, fearful of the sabertooth tiger. Once a tiger passed, our ancestors could relax. Many of us live and act as though our lives are filled with tigers crouching in the shadows just beyond the fire. The rush of adrenalin, heightened reflexes, clamped-down surface blood vessels, and other physiological reactions so useful to meeting a *specific* threat are with many of us most of the time. Those same reactions prepared our ancestors to fight or run. Once the tiger left, these physiological reactions also subsided. And there was often the physical release of combat that served to burn up the biochemicals associated with stress.

We live in a much more complex environment. We have stress producing conditions on all sides. For many of us, the stress reactions never quite depart, leaving us perpetually in a state of readiness to fight or flee. The release of physically attacking the feared or hated source is, of course, usually not available. The result is that the stress-associated chemicals continue to reverberate in our bodies long after the threat is gone.

For many people, the modern equivalent of the jungle is the company or "organization." For many supervisors and managers, the fire at the cave's mouth is their office or plant. And for many, the equivalent of the tiger is their boss, or a higher level of management.

We have substituted for the occasional stress of being near the speed, strength, and ferocity of the tiger, the power of position granted by the organizational hierarchy. Some of us have substituted the boss for the tiger, and our stress reactions to the two are very similar. The difference is that when the occasional tiger departs, so does the threat and the stress. But "the boss" or "the management" doesn't leave. And neither does the stress. Why else is Valium reported to be more often prescribed than all other prescription drugs combined? Why else do so many people find the three-martini lunch essential just to get through the rest of the day?

Many of us have created, elaborated, and even nurtured a menagerie of fears that we permit to hold us back from using our power and influence. To be sure, some of those fears stem from traumatic early life experiences. They may be so severe that professional, therapeutic help is necessary if we are to go beyond fear to freedom. But many of our fears are not that severe or deeply rooted. We have learned and even embraced many fears that we can elect to release and give up. That choice is an expression of our personal power.

Laid-off or terminated employees who elect to leave the security of their city or neighborhood to seek work a continent away are using their personal power. Surely, there is risk and uncertainty in doing so. It can be scary. But it can also enormously enhance one's self-respect.

Perhaps the high rate of separation and divorce is an indication that many people are giving up the fear of being alone. Or perhaps they are giving up a fear that one can't emotionally or financially make it without the security of the family. Maybe they are giving up the fear of social ostracism or anxiety that they will have feelings of intense guilt.

Many marriages fail or are unsatisfying because one or both partners do not use their personal power effectively to gain self-esteem from the relationship. We may not really try to use our power for fear of loss—or we may try and fail. A dissolved relationship may be the end result in either case, but we will feel better about ourselves for having tried.

Just as we do many self-hurtful things to avoid the emotion of fear and to cope with the stress reactions that accompany it, we also do many things to avoid the feeling of guilt and its associated stress. Guilt is really fear once removed. If we think once again of the four sources of self-esteem, we can see that guilt is a result of acting in some way counter to a deeply held value or belief. Guilt arises from fear that others will see us as not worthwhile in some important respect. Even worse is the fear that *we* don't or won't feel ourselves to be valuable. Guilt, too, can be a barrier to the use of our own power.

The husband or wife who engages in an intense extramarital relationship may remain in the marriage and even become a more devoted spouse in an attempt to atone for behavior counter to powerful religious, moral, and ethical values. Such a person is often trying to offset the feelings of guilt and fear, and is attempting to avoid admitting that the marital relationship is a failure. Perhaps he or she is trying to avoid the fear of being found out.

When we permit fear or guilt to paralyze us in the use of our own power to obtain self-esteem, we virtually guarantee ourselves feelings of deep depression, sadness, loneliness, and anger. When we openly admit and consider our fears and guilty feelings, and deliberately choose to become more powerful and influential, we usually feel a great release of strength, energy, and even joy.

This does not mean that one should automatically or immediately seek to use his or her power directly in all situations. For example, it would be foolish to suggest that one should always confront his boss without reflecting on the quality of the relationship, the personality of the boss, and, perhaps, one's marketability and financial condition. To choose *deliberately* not to be confrontive in a particular situation is not necessarily a give-away of one's power. Rather, it may be the careful husbanding of that power for use in a more appropriate circumstance. One might, for example, deliberately assume a low-key stance and elect not to attempt to use power in a no-win work situation. But one might, at the same time, decide to devote one's influence to locating a different employer. This is an appropriate and thoughtful use of personal power. Remaining in the no-win situation because of a host of unrecognized, mythical fears *is* a giveaway of one's power.

Except in unusual circumstances, our personal power cannot be taken away by anyone. But many of us give our power away. We abdicate and suffer a loss in our self-esteem, and we have the predictable feelings of anxiety, anger, hurt, sadness, and loss.

chapter five

How we use and project our power

The way each of us uses personal power and projects influence to meet our need for self-esteem is a highly individual matter. Much of what we mean by the terms "management style" and "personality" is our summary view of the way a particular person uses power. Descriptions like "approachable" or "intimidating," "laid back or charismatic," "sociable" or "aloof," "loyal" or "independent," and many others come to mind when we reflect on the styles and approaches used by the people around us. Any of these descriptions can be viewed as a person's characteristic way of using personal power. Refer back to the description you wrote in chapter one about the approach and style of someone you know. Reflect on your description as you think about the ideas presented in this chapter.

The fact that the ways we use power are important aspects of our individual style and approach should not be surprising. Nor should we be surprised that most of us are fairly good at spotting the ways other people use their power. All of us have had early exposures to the power style of others when we were dependent on them for our basic needs. We saw power in the relationships between our parents and others in the family. We learned something about how to use our power to meet our own needs

FIGURE 5.1. How We Use Our Personal Power.

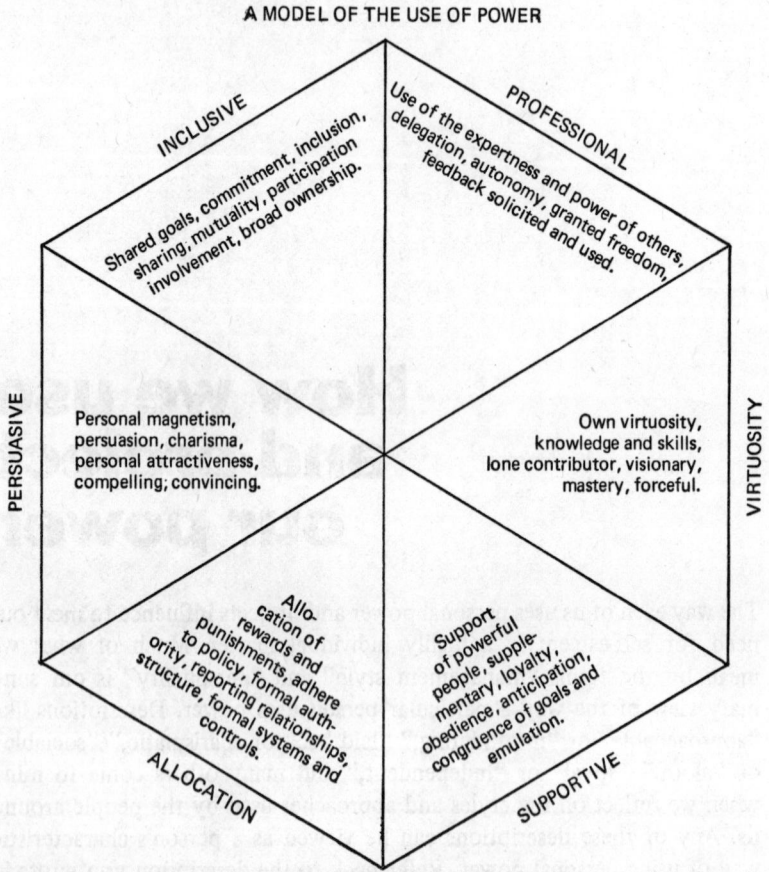

A MODEL OF THE USE OF POWER

INCLUSIVE: Shared goals, commitment, inclusion, sharing, mutuality, participation, involvement, broad ownership.

PROFESSIONAL: Use of the expertness and power of others, delegation, autonomy, granted freedom, feedback solicited and used.

PERSUASIVE: Personal magnetism, persuasion, charisma, personal attractiveness, compelling; convincing.

VIRTUOSITY: Own virtuosity, knowledge and skills, lone contributor, visionary, mastery, forceful.

ALLOCATION: Allocation of rewards and punishments and adhere to policy, formal authority, reporting relationships, structure, formal systems and controls.

SUPPORTIVE: Support of powerful people, supplementary, loyalty, obedience, anticipation, congruence of goals and emulation.

in experiences with our brothers, sisters, parents, teachers, and friends. Since then we have used power to meet our needs and have observed others doing so in a wide variety of relationships and organizations. Figure 5.1 shows some characteristic ways we use our power.

Includer

The includer deliberately and significantly involves others in helping to meet his or her needs. The power and influence of this approach is to have others fully aware of your needs and included in formulating actions intended to help you meet those needs. The influence and power derives from the personal commitment of others to actions that meet your needs. The power also results from the skills of committed people working together as a team. Considerable sharing, receptivity, and mutuality will usually take place. Many ideas and new approaches are typically suggested. Determining new business directions or establishing family financial goals might be examples where others will be invited into the decision process. Everyone involved will know that his contribution and ideas have been explored. A person who uses power in this way will often, and openly, demonstrate that others important to him or her are highly valued and cared about. Achievements, intentions, and personal characteristics may all be favorably noted. Because all of us need expressions of being valued, this way of using one's power increases the self-esteem of others involved. Broad participation characterizes this approach.

Professional

The professional seeks and uses both expert knowledge and the power of others. We would want the most skilled and talented advisors and associates available. So, we would tend to select key subordinates with particular strengths. We would seek and follow the advice of a broad range of professional expertise, counsel, and experience in both personal and career situations. People who use this style will often require status and progress reports from the other experts. They will tend to test out ideas and approaches with a few trusted advisors. Part of the power comes from being the *only* one who has *all* the pertinent information and, clearly, the ultimate authority. A person with this as a primary approach will not only seek out experts, but will also tend to allow them considerable freedom and autonomy in carrying out their functions. The power also comes from having skilled and effective experts each functioning largely autonomously in the service of portions of one's own goals. Clear delegation of accountability *and* authority describe this approach.

Virtuoso

The virtuoso relies primarily on the strength of his or her own drive, expertness, and skills. The individual's power depends on his or her own drive and ability to sort out complexities and come to sound decisions. These are then implemented. Such a person is likely to be a reflective observer and somewhat visionary. Those who use this style often have sublime confidence in their own efficacy and competence, and they usually strive to consistently increase their skills and knowledge. While such a person will make an effort to learn from and work through others, he or she has more inclination to influence events and situations through individual, focused effort. This style relies on the direct application of personal influence to shape events and is much less dependent on the good will or competence of others. Many entrepreneurs use this style. Clarity of personal perception and goals, knowledge, and focused energy characterize this way of using power.

Supporter

The supporter depends on and is effective at winning and holding the support, backing, and sponsorship of others—most especially of influential and powerful people. Such a person tends to be openly supportive of others who are influential. He or she will tend to exhibit loyalty, support, and obedience towards such people and will try to make his or her behavior, goals, and philosophy congruent, and even emulative, of those whose support he or she seeks. Those who use this style most effectively can usually anticipate accurately the desires and reactions of their mentors. The power and influence achieved by using this style is derivative, but it can be considerable when the person is perceived as acting "in the name of", "in concert with", or "at the request of" a powerful and influential person. Imitating the behavior and attitudes of a powerful and effective executive or other mentor can also be an excellent way to learn successful ways to use one's own power in a particular organization. Moreover, with the assured support of powerful people, one is free to exercise considerable independence in the use of one's own power. Loyal support, anticipation, and shared values are key elements.

Allocator

The allocator uses power through more formal structures and mechanisms. Enforced adherence to rules and policies, the allocation of rewards and punishments, and use of standards and control of information are all characteristics of this style. Such a person prefers to use his or her influence unilaterally and at a distance. Power is not expressed through the inclusion of others or through their commitment, but does rely on the power and expertise of others. It is not personal and direct as in the virtuoso style, and is relatively independent of the influence of powerful people, as in the supportive style. In a business situation, this style might be displayed by requiring regular, detailed reports, and audits. Adherence to some set of standards is enforced and expected. Usually there is a well-defined, pyramid-shaped organization structure. Power depends on and is expressed less through personal intervention than through a structure of rules, hierarchical reporting relationships, and specified degrees of authority for each level in the structure. This more formal style requires the power of position and a high degree of control over outcomes.

Persuader

The persuader expresses and projects power through reliance on his or her own magnetism and persuasiveness to cause others to do as he or she wishes. This style depends on the possession of some charisma and personal attractiveness. Verbal fluency, flexibility, and some magnetism are used to project power and influence. This style is as direct as the virtuoso, rather than remote as in the style of the allocator. It does not depend on formal structures and authority. The commitment of others is obtained not so much by the mutual sharing and problem solving of the includer, but by persuasive skills and negotiation. The persuader does not rely on others' desires for freedom and autonomy like the professional style, although he or she may rely on the knowledge, power, and skills of others. People who successfully use this approach typically project a great deal of confidence. They demonstrate considerable energy and a high degree of commitment to some goal or objective. They are often excellent horse traders and adept at sensing others' needs. It also seems that such people are often visibly willing to do less glamorous work than their positions might require.

These seem to be six ways most of us seek to use our personal power. Overall, the six styles seem equally effective; but they are not equally effective in all situations. Most of us have one or perhaps two styles we tend to use most often. The particular approach we use has been adopted because it worked—it enhanced our self-esteem. We can also elect to use other styles. Often just thinking about an upcoming situation will suggest that some style other than our usual one might be more effective. It is also true for most of us that under stress and opposition we will revert to our most preferred approach. We might think about some well-known figures and the way they have seemed to use their power. Most of them, just as most of us, probably used more than one power style. But perhaps one or two styles stand out.

EXERCISE IN USING THE PERSONAL POWER MODEL

Think about the ways the following well-known people seem to have used their power. You may find that they relied on two complementary styles or that they used different approaches at different points in their careers.

1. Reflect on what you know about each person.
2. Refer to the preceding power descriptions.
3. Decide what the individual's primary style seems to have been.
4. Choose which, if any, other styles seem to have been important.

We will examine the power styles of some of these people. Compare your analyses.

TABLE 5.1. Power Styles

PERSON	MAIN STYLE	COMPLIMENTARY OR BACKUP STYLE
General Dwight D. Eisenhower when he was Supreme Allied Commander during World War II		
President Lyndon B. Johnson —As President —Earlier in his career in the U.S. Senate		
General George Patton		
White House Chiefs of Staff		
Top-Level Corporate Executives		
General Robert E. Lee		

General Dwight D. Eisenhower, for example, seems to have used a persuasive style primarily. His charisma and persuasiveness were enormously effective in maintaining a sometimes fragile alliance. President Lyndon B. Johnson also seems to have depended on this style in his later years in the Senate. Earlier in his career, he seems to have relied more on being a supporter as he successfully gained and held the backing of powerful Senators such as Senator Albin Barkley.

General George Patton seems to have projected his personal power through use of his own awesome competency and knowledge as a virtuoso. He regularly read and studied to improve his skill and was supremely confident of his ability.

White House chiefs of staff depend most on the effective use of a supporter style because they require the backing of a powerful person, in this case, the President. They seem to become more powerful if they appear to be an extension of the President. Early in World War II, General Eisenhower seems to have drawn his power from the support of General George Marshall, who selected, promoted, and consistently supported him. Many people in "assistant-to" positions effectively exert far more influence than their organizational level in the hierarchy would suggest. The secretaries of senior-level corporate executives are often very influential for the same reason.

Most sizeable, pyramidal organizations—in business, religion, education, and government—are managed by allocation. This style relies on formal power of position, regulations, clear authority, and, most importantly, the allocation of rewards and punishments. The allocator's style is the least personally involving, drawing power from the existence of outside, more remote mechanisms. It seems the most commonly used style in large organizations.

Examining models of personal power more closely raises the question of whether each of us has only one power style. Most of us do not. Some of us do have one way of projecting our power that is so clear, so strong, and so regularly used that we may appear to have only one style. In fact, most of us have one preferred or dominant way of applying our power, and we *also* have a backup, support, or subordinate style. Very often, our secondary or backup approach is directly opposite to our primary style, as outlined in Figure 5.1.

That is, if you are an includer, your secondary tendency is most probably to be a supporter. The skills and some of the processes are similar. Both seek to have others willingly support actions which will meet our needs. Both require the ability to accurately assess the needs, motives and desires of others. Both depend on some level of interpersonal trust and liking. Both including and supporting are interpersonal approaches.

If your primary power style is professional, your most likely supporting use of your power is allocation. If you prefer to carefully select expert and professional advisors and associates and permit them to autonomously carry out important functions, you will probably want some reporting of their progress, solutions, plans, and accomplishments. You will probably establish or use some fairly regular way of monitoring events. Both of these are more systemic styles.

Both the professional and allocator approaches require a structure that defines positions, expectations, and authority. It is through this structure and system that power is exerted. Top-level executives of large organizations most often view their companies or agencies as a large number of interacting parts that have to be effectively linked. They often see their roles as selecting subordinate managers, distributing resources, providing rewards and incentives, and defining who is to do what. Fundamentally, they define the organization's overall goals and direct the various interlocked elements. Theirs is a systemic view. They view the organization as a complex system which reflects their power.

General Robert E. Lee seems to have relied most on a professional power style. He selected and depended on the expertness and competence of others. He was a somewhat remote, even Olympian figure to all but a very few key subordinates. This is not to ignore his personal magnetism as displayed, for example, in his farewell address, or his deep concern for the plight of the common soldier. Rather, it is to highlight the care with which he selected his subordinate commanders and the freedom he permitted them. Still, he required and even demanded regular, detailed reports from even his most trusted and effective lieutenants. As a key element in his style, Lee regularly used the formal military structure by employing promotions as rewards for achievement. This is the allocation style in action. Contrast Lee's power style with that used by many Union officers throughout most of the Civil War. Few Northern generals were allowed much latitude. The dominant force was the military and political hierarchy and the application of policy, rules, and procedures. One result is that the average person can probably name more Southern than Northern generals. Although both the professional and allocation approaches are more personally remote, structural styles, they differ very significantly.

If yours is a virtuoso style, your most predictable secondary approach is persuasion. Both approaches represent a personal use of one's power and influence. For example, the German Field Marshall, Erwin Rommel, may have been the most skillful battlefield commander of World War II. While commanding the Afrika Korps, he nearly always lacked sufficient men, supplies, and tanks while opposing the overwhelming strength of a well-supplied enemy. Although he was audacious, creative, and bold, Rommel never needlessly sacrificed his men. From all accounts, Rommel was dedicated to proper and humane treatment for both his men and prisoners. He led by vigorous example, persuasion, and dash. His troops had an enormous regard for him. In Rommel we may see a practitioner of personal virtuosity and skill supported or backed up by persuasion and charisma.

In each of these three situations the reverse style linkage is also probable. That is, if you are a supporter, your secondary way of using power is likely to be inclusion. Below are the three major power categories showing the two styles that are often used as backup approaches for each other.

An example of the three major orientations might be the responses of three different people faced with the job of building a long bridge over a deep chasm in difficult terrain. A person who prefers a personal power style might say:

> I can clearly visualize how the bridge should be constructed and am completely confident I can build it.

The interpersonal approach might be:

> Together we can develop a plan and design based on the best thinking of us all. Together, we can build it.

A systemic use of power might be reflected by:

> Our organization has the engineering people and the soils experts. With these skills they can design and build the bridge.

38 / How We Use and Project Our Power

Interpersonally Powerful

Includer	Supporter
Affiliative	Approachable
Aware	Sensitive
Loyal	Collaborative
Encouraging	Empowering (others)

Focus: On others
Example: A coach

Personally Powerful

Virtuoso	Persuader
Autonomous	Charismatic
Persuasive	Masterful
Visionary	Expert
Independent	Confident

Focus: On self
Example: A player

Systematically Powerful

Professional	Allocator
Planning	Orderly
Delegating	Directive
Distributing	Coordinated
Formal	Remote

Focus: The system
Example: The team manager

To review in summary form:

1. A positive sense of self-worth and value—of self-esteem—is critical to each of us.
2. Experience and events early in our lives influence our self-esteem, but many present situations and conditions also impact how we feel about ourselves.

3. Power is not only one of the four sources of self-esteem, it is also the energizer that allows us to gain positive feelings of self-worth and value from the world around us.

4. Much of a person's uniqueness, visible behavior and approach to life, even his personality, is intimately bound up with his or her particular use of power. Whether or not and how we use our power is very often a matter of choice. We can learn to use our power in a variety of ways, thereby increasing the likelihood of gaining positive self-esteem.

5. Personal power can be *given* away or ignored, but except in unusual cases it cannot be taken away. That is why *we* are in charge of our self-esteem.

6. There appear to be six distinctive ways of using or employing one's personal power. Most people seem to have a dominant or primary approach and a backup or secondary style. Two styles are basically *personal* in nature, two are *interpersonal*, and two are *systemic*.

REFLECTIONS ON THE WAY *YOU* USE POWER

Look back to Figure 5.1. Think about how you are most likely to use your power in various situations. Remember, the style directly across the circle from your most likely approach is probably your secondary or backup way of using your power.

Below are listed a number of interpersonal and organization situations. Select the situations that seem to fit your recent experience. Try to select conditions you've experienced in the last few months and can clearly remember. Beside each situation you've selected, pick the style that best describes what you did and how you used or tried to use your power. How did you seek to influence the situation?

Situation	Style
1. A disagreement with your spouse on a moderately important issue.	
2. A planning meeting with your boss where you are setting goals and objectives.	

Situation	Style

3. A meeting about a major problem in your area of responsibility where your boss, other senior level managers, and your peers are present.
4. Reprimanding your child for some improper behavior.
5. A meeting where you feel your department is being criticized.
6. Discussing school work problems with your child.
7. Discussing a major purchase of something you want but your spouse does not.
8. Holding a performance review or appraisal with a subordinate.
9. Determining the goals and objectives of your department or group for the next year.
10. Considering with your spouse how to best educate your children.
11. Working to solve a significant personal problem.
12. Working to solve a major business or professional problem.
13. There is conflict because what you very much want to do is opposed by another.
14. Two of your children are having a noisy argument.
15. Two of your subordinates are locked in a significant dispute.
16. Your teacher or professor gives you a much lower grade on an important exam than you think you deserve.
17. As a supervisor or manager, the union makes demands you think are completely unreasonable.
18. Your fourteen-year-old-child has walked away from home for the second time in a few months.
19. Despite a lot of hard work and long hours, your boss has just evaluated your work performance as only marginal.

Situation   *Style*

20. Something you want very much to do will cost a lot of money. You are about to meet with some possible lenders.

If you are like many people, you will probably find that one or two power styles stand out. Consider your preferred use of power. Are there other styles that may have been more effective? Are there some styles you rarely use? Could these styles be useful?

chapter six

The six power styles and self-esteem

For most of us, the choice of a style for expressing our power was learned long ago. Indeed, recognizing and using our power was probably one of the first things we learned simply because of its intimate connection and importance to our self-respect. We have always needed our power to gain those all-important, positive feelings about who and what we are as unique human beings. These feelings are summed up by the terms self-esteem and self-respect.

Without the use of our personal power, esteem income that comes our way from the four sources is largely a matter of chance. And most of us need *far* more affirmative, self-confirming feelings about ourselves than chance is likely to supply. So we have learned to use and exert our power. With age and experience, success and failure, and joy and misery, we have developed a rich diversity in the ways we use our power.

Still, if we reflect on our own behaviors and closely observe those around us, we will see that there are six styles or types of personal influence and power, as described in Chapter Five. But why and how do we select and rely primarily upon a particular way of using our personal power? We generally select the power style, or mix of styles, that in the

43

past has been most effective in gaining positive feelings about ourselves from a preferred source of self-esteem. One style or another simply worked best.

For the longer term, we need esteem income from all four of the major sources. For the short range, and when esteem from one or another source is not available, we compensate by striving for increased esteem from the remaining sources to keep our tank reasonably full (Table 2.1). Probably beginning in very early life we obtained more good and positive feelings about ourselves from one source than another. So we learned what felt good. We became more skillful at using our power in ways to gain positive feelings from *that* particular source. In some cases, however, a severe lack of esteem in early life may lead us now to vigorously seek esteem from one or another source that was missing before. Many people try to make up in the present for a painful absence in the past.

For example, early success in learning to feed ourselves may have brought praise from our parents and an exhilarating feeling of independence and competence. We found that taking some risk could be fun. Achievement and accomplishment, then, might have become a preferred source of self-esteem. And so we learned to use our personal power to obtain esteem from achievement.

Or, as very young children, we might have experienced much touching, holding, and cuddling that gave us a sense of warmth, comfort, and security. We felt cared about, valued, and important to someone who was important to us. We may also have been praised for expressing affection and caring for others. And so, evidence of being cared about and valued became our preferred source of self-esteem. To receive esteem from this source, we learned particular ways of using our personal power.

A very successful entrepreneur friend of mine apparently did not feel valued or cared about as a youngster. Over the years, he has revealed small pieces of what must have been a lonely, awfully unhappy childhood. He felt unwanted, rejected, insecure, and an outcast even from close members of his family. It isn't hard to see how that terribly hurt little boy decided to use his power as an adult to make sure that no one could hurt him again. Power itself became an obsession, and a fortune its expression. He did not want money for the things it could buy or to support some notable achievement. Money was, to him, literally the power to make others act as he wished. He used it as both a carrot and a stick. If positive feelings from being cared about could not be gained, at least negative expressions could be avoided through the use of his power.

As a young child, you may very early have demonstrated vigorous exploratory behaviors that led you to manipulate objects all around your small world. You may have been praised, admired, and shown off to others for crawling or walking. It isn't hard to see how such events may have led to an intense desire for self-respect, especially from the use of your own, individual power, however limited it might have been at the time.

Notions of right and wrong surround many children. At first we were rewarded for "good" behavior and punished for being "bad." Later, we may have overheard conversations, been exposed to a religious atmosphere, and begun to emulate some aspects of the value system we sensed in the environment. Many teenagers rebel against these early values, but a large number return to values and ethics fairly congruent with those experienced as children. Behaving in accordance with one's values, ethics, and beliefs might, then, become a primary source of esteem.

Power, as we have noted, is a *source* of self-esteem and *also* the energizing factor enabling self-esteem to be gained from the world around us. Power serves two functions. Our values, codes, and belief systems also seem to serve a dual role. Acting in accordance with our most basic beliefs directly enhances our self-esteem. But behaviors congruent with our values are more than self-esteem builders. Our values and beliefs provide direction and guidance to our efforts to gain self-esteem. As an analogy, think of a motorboat. Power is like the engine propelling our efforts to gain self-esteem; our values and beliefs are like the rudder guiding and directing those efforts.

The six power styles often seem to be linked with one or another preferred source of self-esteem. That is, the particular component of self-esteem most important to us seems to be related to the power style we use to get the self-respect we need so greatly.

For example, when we work with managers and supervisors who admit to a strong desire to be cared about and valued, we typically see them use either an inclusion or a supportive power style. If they are appropriately skilled, they tend to involve peers and subordinates in many planning, goal-setting, informational, and review sessions. If they are less skilled, they will do a lot of talking with others but with a lower organizational payoff. In either case, their power comes from the commitment of those around them. At a self-esteem level, they feel valued, desired, and cared about by being involved in such activities. Remember, we can't see self-esteem. Only with reflection and questioning do we become aware of our own needs for self-respect. But we can and do see power behaviors.

People who develop especially close relationships with their bosses typically express loyalty and support toward them. They defend the boss's actions to others. They anticipate his or her desires and derive their power from the boss. People in "assistant-to" and other staff positions often use a supportive style. They feel good about themselves, valued, and cared about by being included and closely linked to a powerful or influential person. But this power style is hardly limited to those in "assistant-to" positions. It is in common use in almost every organization and many families. Mothers sometimes don't use their own power with their children. They threaten unruly children with the power of their father. This reduces the mother's power and, therefore, her overall self-esteem.

In 1588, King Philip II of Spain appointed the Duke of Medina Sidonia to manage and command the Spanish Armada then being assembled and built at Lisbon. The new Captain-General took over from the recently deceased Marquis of Santa Cruz. Santa Cruz, a renowned naval hero and commander, had tried to manage and control each facet of the enormous enterprise himself. From all accounts he enjoyed the exercise of power for its own sake. Medina Sidonia had no such base of experience: He was appointed for reasons other than his skills as a naval commander. This modest man had, however, proven himself a most able administrator.

Under Santa Cruz, the results were chaotic. Crews, guns, provisions, and clothing were almost hopelessly confused, and Philip wanted no delay in attacking England. Medina Sidonia formed a staff of able, experienced, and well-recommended captains to compensate for his own weaknesses. He, in turn, used his considerable administrative skills to implement many of his staff's recommendations. The staff work was far more effective and far less acrimonious than it had been under Santa Cruz. There is evidence that a considerable amount of warmth existed within the staff that spread beyond that small nucleus.

Although there seems to have been no question that Medina Sidonia was in charge, he sought and deferred to the judgments of others. It seems clear that he greatly valued and drew substantial energy and support from his tightly knit team. The results were dramatic. While it is unlikely that any commander or any fleet could have accomplished Philip's objectives, there is little question that the Armada that sailed was a vastly improved fleet over the one Santa Cruz had assembled.

Medina Sidonia deliberately shared power. He included his subordinates in virtually every important decision and frequently deferred to their judgment. He seems to have deliberately attempted to reach a consensus on major issues. In this way the vast enterprise became manageable and the strengths of the key participants more effectively used. From what little we know, the new Captain-General very much enjoyed being valued, accepted, and involved with his subordinate commanders. He and his men drew strength from the relationship.

The way Santa Cruz used power, through personal virtuosity and mastery, may have been entirely appropriate to a much smaller task. Medina Sidonia's style, inclusion, seems to have been very effective in dealing with such an enormous undertaking as the outfitting and command of the Armada. Each seems to have used a power style oriented to gaining personal self-esteem from a preferred source.

It seems, then, that if being valued and cared about is an especially important source of self-esteem, we will tend to use inclusive or supportive power behaviors to get the esteem we need.

The personally shattering effects of divorce are frequently so devastating because self-esteem from being valued and cared about is drastically reduced. If that is, in fact, the most important source of esteem for an individual, we would expect the use of personal power to reflect that need. Similarly, a person who has had little esteem income from that source outside of the family, may now feel a great loss in self-respect and personal worthiness. We would expect his or her personal power to be used in Inclusive and/or Supportive ways. Perhaps this explains why so many groups and organizations exist that are oriented to helping recently divorced people meet one another.

If personal achievement of goals *you* set or are committed to is a major source of good feelings for you, you will tend to use your personal power to obtain self-esteem primarily from that source. When faced with a painful reduction in self-esteem, you might put a great deal of energy into a favorite hobby or get involved in some project. You will tend to actively pursue some visible accomplishment.

Characteristically, such people try to influence their personal, social, physical, or professional environments by using the power styles we've labelled virtuoso or persuasive. These power styles are *personally* "close," while the inclusive and supportive approaches considered earlier are *interpersonally* "close." The Expert or Formality modes are more institutional, more remote, more *systemic* and *structural*.

Visible achievement and accomplishment of one's goals is a very personal event. It is often not necessary that others be aware of the achievement. The positive, self-worth confirming feelings of achievement are ultimately internal and private and are not dependent on the approval of others. It is no surprise to find that people whose primary source of self-esteem is accomplishment tend to use their power in personal ways. If you are such a person, you will tend to use a virtuoso or persuasive approach to get what you need: positive feelings of self-esteem.

Recall that our personal use of power and influence is learned, and that we often tend to use paired styles. That is, if virtuoso behaviors do not succeed for you in obtaining self-esteem from visible achievement, you will tend to use a persuasive backup approach. The reverse is also true.

In 1796, Napoleon Bonaparte, under the command of the Directory, was just beginning his renowned career and the Italian campaign. At Nice, where his army had gathered, he first became aware of a terrible state of disorganization. There was no money, virtually no means of transportation, and essentially no food. In two days, Napoleon secured a week's rations for the entire army and 12,000 pairs of shoes—all by his own energy and knowledge. When called before the Committee of Safety earlier he had taken just a half-hour and two sheets of paper to describe the detailed plan for the successful Italian campaign. He had already used his enormous skill and intuition to develop a full plan, which he implemented a few months later.

In Italy, substantial units of his army were largely undisciplined. Discipline and pride were rapidly established, and the "undisciplined brigands" became some of the best soldiers in the world. To establish a sense of identity, discipline, and morale in the army, he regularly moved among his soldiers, informally stimulating and questioning them. While other commanders speak to their troops, few have done so with such crisp vividness as Napoleon. There was a magnetic persuasiveness in his words that stirred and welded the men to him.

Achievement clearly seems to have been Napoleon's goal, at least early in his career. He longed to win battles, to defeat some renowned foe, and to obtain great rewards and treasure for France. He used the paired power styles of personal virtuosity and persuasion, depending on the need. Napoleon seems not to have greatly valued or needed the caring of other people. Several accounts describe him as often working entirely alone, oblivious to a room full of officers and dignitaries seeking his attention or favor. His seems to have been a solitary, visionary style of using power supported by a charismatic persuasiveness when direct commands would not succeed and when he needed the commitment of thousands of others to implement his schemes.

Like most successful leaders, however, Napoleon used other power styles on occasion. He could be lavish in bestowing praise, rewards, and promotions through the more formal use of his power. Once a particular commander gained Napoleon's confidence, he would permit that officer unusual autonomy and freedom. Thus, he sometimes relied on a professional power style. Still, in difficult circumstances, he nearly always seems to have used either his personal mastery and virtuosity or to have relied on his own persuasive magnetism. Achievements were his goals and virtuosity the way he used his power to gain his goals.

If the exercise of power and influence over people and situations is the major source of positive feelings about yourself, you will probably tend to use professional or allocation approaches. In the typical organizational pyramid these are frequent ways of projecting one's power. Most organizations are highly structured, rather authoritarian, and pyramidal. Social structures have long had these characteristics. For example, the family has traditionally been headed by a father, the state by a king, the Catholic Church by a Pope, and the company by a president. Each of us has had lifelong experiences with such social structures. The higher we are able to climb in such organizations, the more we have control over the organization's wealth and power. It is not surprising, then, that the exercise of power over people and events is the major source of self-esteem for so many of us.

We will use our own influence in characteristic ways to be able to get the power and control over people and events we need to feel good about ourselves. Typically, we use the allocation or professional modes. In the allocation approach, one's power comes partially by controlling the behavior of others through rewards and punishments. Formal, position-based authority and the use of various reporting and control systems are key elements. Through these mechanisms, the behavior of many others can be influenced, directed, and controlled. In using the professional style, our power derives from the expert, skilled performance and knowledge of carefully selected subordinates and advisors who are allowed considerable latitude in their individual, professional roles. And our power is also a result of being the only one with all of the information and the power of final decision. In this style, the expert advisors are influential particularly in their respective areas. Full knowledge and ultimate power remains at the top of the department, family, church, or company. This systemic use of our personal influence relies more on the use of structure, authority, and control than on personal or interpersonal techniques.

To briefly return to an earlier example, the English queen, Elizabeth I, seems to have used quite a different approach to preparing her fleet for battle than the Spanish. Elizabeth had earlier permitted, supported, and encouraged the individual expertise of men like John Hawkins who redesigned, built, and repaired her ships. The result was an able fleet, faster and more maneuverable than any before it. She permitted equally great freedom to William Wynter who used his expertise to successfully arm the new ships in equally revolutionary ways. The results were ships that at longer ranges could decisively outgun any foe.

Hawkins and Wynter were rivals, and sometimes enemies. But as collaborators, they were permitted by Elizabeth to use their own skills and power with considerable autonomy in their fields of expertise. Elizabeth kept hold on the purse strings and mediated. She alone had the final say and control of the resources. She used largely a professional style in projecting her power.

The relationship between a particular self-esteem source and the most likely personal power approach seems fairly clear for achieving, for gaining power and control, and for feeling cared about. It is not so clear when we examine ethical and moral dilemmas. The plant manager described in Chapter Two used several power styles in trying to change what he felt were the unethical, immoral actions of his company. Some people use all six styles and mixtures of styles in trying to cope with actions, situations, or behaviors that violated their sense of ethics and morality.

To solve the problem with others, some seek to use others' expertise or delegate the matter, and others use a high degree of personal magnetism and persuasion. If the issue is serious enough to the individual, and his characteristic approaches to power and influence fail, he or she will most likely resort to a virtuoso approach and attempt to force the issue toward a personal vision of proper resolution.

As we have seen, this use of power relies on the strength of our individual drive, skills, and ability. Such an approach involves influencing events and situations through personal, focused efforts. In a severe enough conflict about values, morality or ethics, most of us will ultimately either confront the issue head-on, leave the situation, or both. Thus, virtuosity is probably the ultimate backup style when our self-esteem is threatened by conflicts in our most basic ethics and beliefs.

To summarize:

1. The particular source of self-esteem that is now individually the most important to us grew to be enormously significant in early childhood and became a part of who we are largely as a result of relationships in the home.

2. We use our personal power to gain positive feelings about ourselves, to feel worthwhile and valuable. We use our power to gain self-esteem.

3. Without the use of our power, most of us will not experience adequately affirmative feelings that confirm our self-worth.

4. The specific *way* we generally use our personal power was probably learned as children and modified by our experiences in the home, church, school, with friends, and in our work lives.

5. We tend to use our power in one or more of six individualistic ways, largely influenced by the particular source of self-esteem that is most important to us. But most of us need positive esteem income from all four sources.

6. The relationships between our individual self-esteem requirements and the particular kinds of power behaviors we tend to use to meet those needs are shown in Table 6.1.

TABLE 6.1. Power and the Sources of Self-Esteem

ESTEEM SOURCE:	MOST LIKELY OR CHARACTERISTIC PERSONAL POWER STYLE:	
1. Successful application of influence, control, and power.	Allocation	Professional
2. Achievement and accomplishment of personally important goals.	Virtuoso	Persuasive
3. Evidence of being cared about and valued.	Inclusive	Supportive
4. Behaving in accordance with our cherished values and beliefs.	All, but ultimately the virtuoso style.	

… chapter seven

Overuse of one's power style

Thus far we have considered six primary ways we express and use our personal power to get the self-respect we all require. The six approaches can be equally effective; there is no single best way to express one's power. But each of the six basic power styles *can* be overused, with a negative impact on our self-esteem.

For example, a business manager who uses the inclusive approach gains power from the committed involvement and contributions of those around him or her. They are included, their views are sought and heard, and they have influence when mutually determined plans, assignments, and strategies are implemented. Clearly, this is a powerfully effective use of personal power because the manager gains self-esteem. It is also effective in meeting the company's goals. But the same style can be so overused that the group, department or organization becomes almost a social club. Somehow, the time slips by without decisions being taken or plans completed. Since the group's members have no clear sense of direction, commitment, or expectations and did not *really* influence future events, they will be frustrated. The manager's self-esteem will suffer because there is no evidence of group commitment and consensus. The organization's performance will also suffer in such a situation. The manager overused his or her preferred approach.

To an observer, the difference between the productive use of an inclusive style and its overuse is clear. In the one case, we are struck by the strong give and take, active listening, involvement, creativity, and even excitement as issues are raised openly, candidly discussed, and solutions are reached or plans agreed upon. In the other case, there is a sense of floundering and of aimlessness. Everyone is physically present, but not really contributing or involved. There is much talk, but no real energy, persistence, or direction. Usually there is little real listening. And the session ends about where it started. This is overuse of the inclusive approach. It is really powerless participation. The manager, in this particular case, has lost sight of the fact that to gain personal feelings of worth and value, there must be a sense of group commitment, movement, and accomplishment. In overusing a preferred approach, the manager has given away the power to gain self-esteem and to have a productive session.

These examples highlight an important point. The very power style that can be a major strength and asset can, if overused, become a weakness and liability. When we use our preferred style excessively, to the exclusion of other styles or in inappropriate circumstances, that style can become completely ineffective. Under stress or opposition, many of us will tend to overuse the style that is normally our most effective. Under such overuse conditions, we actually lose or give away our power and influence. Paradoxical as it may seem, overuse of a strength can become a weakness.

Most effective leaders seem to successfully avoid this trap at least most of the time. They tend to switch to another way of using their power, or even deliberately decide to exercise little influence at all for the present. Ineffective use or giving away one's power will result *both* in reduced opportunity for obtaining personal self-esteem *and*, in a leadership situation, will also result in less effective group and organization performance.

Or, consider the supportive use of power. Clearly, supporting, anticipating, and defending an influential figure can provide you with evidence of being cared about and valued, and can provide esteem from the other sources, too. Consider the position of White House Chief of Staff. It is an essential position, many believe, to husband the President's time and energy. Anyone in such a position is almost certain to have the respect and affection of the President. The power of the Chief of Staff derives from that of the President. He controls, at least partially, access to the President. And he is often presumed to speak in the President's name.

In a business organization, being supportive and loyal to one's supervisor or other powerful figure can also produce feelings of personal worth and value. As a subordinate, it feels good to have the trust, caring, and respect of a more powerful person. So a supportive approach can result in self-esteem *and* a more effective organization. But we have probably all seen an overuse of this way of expressing one's personal power. Sometimes, the subordinate begins to act as if *he or she* has the power independent of the influential figure. Usually, this overuse will not be tolerated. The subordinate will find himself "locked out," and his power will rapidly decline as others realize it.

The subordinate may also become a toady and lose the very respect and caring he needs. An overuse of this often effective application of personal power also usually results in a reduction in the individual's self-esteem *and* a less effective performance. This overuse often appears to others to be excessively political or manipulative. In organizations where "company politics" are often mentioned, the real meaning of the term is usually that there is widespread overuse of the supportive approach.

Selecting and using highly skilled professionals who are given considerable latitude in their respective areas can be very esteem-producing. This is the professional style of using one's power. You retain control and direction of the overall effort because you alone have all the information. This style can produce impressive results. Indeed, this is probably the kind of approach that comes to mind for most people when they think of business, industry, medical clinics, law firms, and many other organizations. We tend to think of many such enterprises as organized around the principles of expertness and delegation of authority.

Here, too, overuse of the professional way of using one's personal power amounts to a giveaway of that power. Overuse can often be seen in organizations of all sizes where the various groups, departments, and functional managers have little knowledge of what others are doing. Organization objectives are unclear in such situations because the various parts and members of the organization are essentially isolated both from each other and from the organization's strategies and goals. The result can be ineffective individual and organization performance because virtually all decisions are made at the top. Often there is much upward delegation of even minor decisions because no one has enough information to decide.

For example, even the presence of excellent individual football players does not necessarily mean a winning season. The essential ingredient is teamwork, which overuse of the professional style often restricts.

For another example, one project-oriented, highly technical organization has a staff consisting largely of young people who hold M.S. and Ph.D. degrees in technical disciplines such as mathematics and computer science. The managers are also young and technically oriented. The organization's power style was described by a top level company executive as: "Find, carefully select, and employ the brightest technical people you can find. Don't worry how much they cost. Give them some broad outlines of the project and leave them alone." This is an overuse of the professional style. It amounts almost to abdication. In many private discussions one staff member after another and most of the young managers said they badly wanted more direction and guidance. They felt little identity with their project or the company, and they felt increasingly cut off from other portions of the project. As they described it, delivery dates and budget projections were both missed because of the overuse of the professional style, which might be called isolated and dependent. Unexpected dependency can develop when someone steps in and uses his or her power to fill the vacuum. At that point the organization can accidentially become dependent on direction from an unknown, unselected, and unaccountable leader. The feelings of isolation can easily develop when there are small groups or individuals who are dependent on each other for success, but who have little sense of mutual sharing, direction, or guidance.

Each of the styles we use to project our personal power can be effective in providing the self-esteem we all need. And each can be overused in a way that amounts to the giving away of our power. Consider the virtuoso approach. If overused, some of us can become arrogant, dogmatic, and obsessed. Others may become so visionary as to become impractical. In the first case, the rigidity can cause us to fail to achieve and accomplish our important goals because we have lost the flexibility of thought, or ceased to improve the knowledge and skills essential to achievement. And by losing the ability to accomplish, we damage our self-esteem. This dogmatic and rigid way of using our personal power results both in less achievement and less self-esteem. Moreover, the visionary drive and knowledge that so often attracts others to rally around someone using the virtuoso power style becomes unattractive when it becomes dogmatic and insensitive.

In some situations the leader gathers so much domination and control, using even senior executives as errand boys, that the organization flounders. As subordinates and the organization uncontrollably squander time and resources, the leader loses the very control and power he or she needs to experience positive feelings. His or her self-esteem suffers as the organization falters.

In the early years of Nazi Germany, Adolf Hitler seems to have been far more inclined to listen to his advisors, both military and civil, than later in the war. Toward the end of the conflict he attempted to personally control and direct individual battles, new weapons development, and economic matters. He was certain of his skill and vision. He issued preemptory orders to many military commanders preventing them from exercising their own judgment. In some cases the results were disastrous defeats. Rigid dogmatism will rarely succeed in the face of rapidly changing conditions.

The allocation approach to using personal power is usually organized, coordinated, and planned. It can be a most effective style, as shown by the rise of many large and productive organizations. To be used successfully, the allocator must have resources to command and be able to control important outcomes. But when carried to extremes, this use can become rigid, autocratic, and dictatorial. It can result in organization members becoming withdrawn from each other and from their superiors; and it can encourage a mindless adherence to rules and regulations. This is an autocratic and remote style in which teamwork suffers, and the self-esteem of both the leader and the members plummet. The leader in such a situation actually has very little real influence. The federal bureaucracy might be an example where even the President and Cabinet members often have only minor influence on the bureaucracy. Rules, procedures and regulations can become so entrenched that adherence to them becomes the organization's real, if unspoken, objective. Leaders can find themselves essentially powerless in such situations. The president of a multi-billion dollar company once angrily described his huge organization as:

> This damn beast. It's like a dragon. I kick it in the head but it is five years before it feels it in its tail.

Finally, the persuasive and charismatic way of exerting one's influence can, as we have seen, be highly effective. Sometimes, however, the style is overused and becomes messianic, demagogic, and haranguing. This *personally* close power style, when overused, can make others so uncomfortable that they pull away and avoid. The overuse by others of a persuasive power style can make us feel very suspicious, and even manipulated. We wonder why such a hard sell is needed. What is *really* in the bottle of snake oil we are being persuaded to buy?

Ideas, actions, and things can all be very effectively advanced through personal magnetism and charismatic persuasion. And all three can lose their attractiveness if that style is overused. In an organizational context, followers will eventually tune out and ignore messianic exhortations, and those who use such an approach will find that they actually have less real power, not more. For example, many political figures with considerable persuasive skill and personal attractiveness begin to overuse their strength as the campaign wears on or their standing in the polls changes. The result can be that the individual begins to lose the very power he seeks. President Lyndon B. Johnson had a commanding lead over Senator Barry Goldwater in the 1964 presidential contest. The President had shown himself to be an attractive, persuasive candidate. Even so, one of his paid political advertisements, depicting a little girl and a mushroom cloud, was clearly seen as demagogic. It probably hurt Johnson, as did some of his almost strident speeches about the Vietnam War.

Table 7.1 lists the effective and ineffective (overuse) approaches to using personal power and influence.

Effectiveness means two different but related outcomes. The effective use of personal power and influence usually means a better performing group or organization because it leaves space for others to improve their

TABLE 7.1 Effective and Ineffective Uses of Personal Power

EFFECTIVE USE:		INEFFECTIVE (OVERUSE):
Inclusive	vs.	Participative/Uncommitted
Supportive	vs.	Political/Manipulative
Professional	vs.	Isolated/Dependent
Virtuoso	vs.	Dogmatic/Obsessed
Allocating	vs.	Autocratic/Remote
Persuasive	vs.	Messianic/Demagogic

own self-esteem. An ineffective use usually results in a decline of organization vitality and performance. But there's more to the effective use of our power than its organization impact. When we use our power effectively, we feel good about who and what we are. An effective use of our personal power means improved self-esteem for ourselves; an ineffective use eventually decreases our sense of self-worth and value.

An Exercise in Studying Self-Esteem and the Use of Personal Power

One of our clients is a large automobile dealership occupying a modern facility in a downtown business section. Strategically situated near several large and expanding population centers, the dealership sells a popular line of relatively high priced automobiles. It employs sixteen salesmen and sixty-six other people, all of whom seem to understand that the success of the dealership depends on the volume and quality of the deals it makes. The owner sought our help because of severe problems in the sales force. The task confronting management, as the owner described it, was to train and motivate salesmen in activities that sell rather than activities that do not produce both volume and good profit deals. If you were to walk into this organization you would probably notice people in the sales area working intently at their desks. You might also see one or more small groups of people talking quietly together.

The dealership has a long history. It was set up by the grandfather of the present owner as a wagon manufacturing and sales facility. Founded in 1881, it became an automobile dealership in the 1920s. Carl Duke III (not his real name) is now president of the family-owned company. Philip Del Rio, Duke's brother-in-law, is sales manager for the company. Five years ago the company hired Bill Reynolds, a college-trained finance and administration director. Reynolds had automobile sales experience as well as experience in accounting and personnel procedures. The personnel policies and practices of the company are established. The company has used employee attitude surveys in the past. It has adequate job descriptions for all major positions in the organization, and a performance evaluation procedure for wage and salary administration and control. The company has a firm training policy and manualized training procedures administered by Reynolds. For sales training, Reynolds provides visual aids and training materials to Del Rio for use in daily sales meetings. These kinds of practices are common in successful dealerships.

The company has had rigid requirements for salesmen (all were male) for the last few years. It has a reputation throughout the territory for its hard-hitting sales force, although employee turnover has been a growing problem. Specified minimum daily requirements are given to new salesmen and discussed with them before they are hired. At the final interview with the applicant, the position description of a salesman and the minimum daily requirement activities sheet are reviewed with him so that he will understand that the job requires a great deal of work with very significant rewards possible, and that what he does will be controlled by the sales manager's office. The minimum daily requirements consist of the following:

1. Each salesman will be required to spend a total of twenty hours a week on the floor of the sales room. His activities on the floor are controlled.
2. Each will make six phone calls per day to prospects during his floor time.
3. Each salesman will make eight additional telephone calls per day to prospects. Some of the names and numbers are obtained through acquaintances of the salesman who are paid a fee by the salesman for each lead that results in a sale. These calls are made in addition to those made during floor time.
4. Each salesman will make five in-person calls per week on prospects by door-to-door or house-to-house canvasses.
5. Each salesman will address and mail twenty pieces per week to prospects. These mailing pieces are prepared cards or letters.
6. The salesman will attend a daily sales meeting beginning at 8:15 A.M. and ending at 9 A.M. five days a week.
7. Each salesman will close at least three deals a week, or
8. He will present a prepared checklist of his activities during the preceding day at the sales meeting.

These minimum daily sales activities requirements may seem high, but the managers feel that they have been found to pay off handsomely for both the company and the salesman. Historically, the salesmen have not objected to the requirements. They seem to have believed that the requirements were, in general, well-founded. Of late, however, there has been significant griping on the part of the salesmen because of the rigid system. Some have said, "Who knows what other things might work better?" Union organizing activity has been steadily growing in the area with some evidence that at least a few company salesmen have been contacted. Union "show of interest" cards have been seen in the dealership.

Of the sixteen salesmen on the payroll of the company, only about half are doing a satisfactory job. Others are making poor and infrequent sales. Four of the salesmen are outstanding, maintaining an average volume of sales of eighteen cars per month. The salesmen are compensated on the basis of a rather liberal direct commission plan. The lower seven of the salesmen are overdrawn against future earnings, with the bottom four overdrawn an excessive amount.

Evaluation of each member of the sales staff who isn't making the sales objective is done in a meticulous manner. A clerk has worked with Reynolds for several years in developing forms and procedures for evaluation. The cumulative number of sales are kept in a record folder for each salesman as well as an index of the profit on the deals he makes. Some counselling between the sales manager's assistant and the salesmen is done, and during these sessions the cumulative records are frequently reviewed. In addition, objective monthly ratings are made by lead men in the sales department and by the sales manager. In general, there is adequate reliability of information concerning relative performance of salesmen.

Duke and Del Rio are dissatisfied with the performance of about half of the salesmen and concerned about the prospect of a union campaign. Duke's numerous sessions with Del Rio and Reynolds have ended with little resolution and some disagreement. Each feels the other is at fault. Duke quite literally grew up in the business. He says of the current sales department procedures and problems:

> My father did damn well by running things with only quotas and a close personal touch with each salesman. I admit we're larger now and maybe I've let Phil do things his way too much. But he *has* in the past gotten good results for me. It's not easy with a member of the family, but his rigid rules are the problem. He's hungry for a piece of this business, too. I'm afraid he's just too tight and rigid. It's better not to let how I feel be too obvious; it could make things worse. Still, we've got to upgrade the performance of half our sales force.

Not surprisingly, Del Rio sees the issues somewhat differently. In a private conversation his feelings became clearer:

> Damn it! If you don't tie some of these guys down with rules and procedures, they'd never close any deals. We'd have curbstoning[1] and things like that which were all over this place before the rules went in. In fact, I'd like to add a requirement that salesmen leave a specified number of offers to trade on windshields of parked cars. You don't hear our top salesmen complain, just the nonproducers. We ought to get rid of some, but Carl's sort of grown up with some of them and won't do it. He's afraid of how people in the community would react, too. I'm supposed to be the sales manager, but Carl is *really* the sales manager in lots of ways.

Reynolds feels uncomfortable that the top people in the dealership are not agreed on some basic approaches. As he says:

> Look, some salesmen have quit. Now, some I didn't mind losing one bit, but we've lost a couple of good ones, too. I'm afraid we could lose more. The union thing worries me. That could really tie our hands, increase costs, and put us at a competitive disadvantage with other dealers in the area. I think maybe both Carl and Phil are partly right and partly wrong in their approach. Whenever we discuss it, Phil gets hot, Carl tries to act cool, but he's upset, too. And here I am—the only nonfamily member in the group. I wish to hell those guys would get together and settle it. I've given them the tools to track and reward performance, but I can't run the whole place.

Study Questions:

1. What are the self-esteem needs of the salesmen? Of Reynolds? Del Rio? Duke?

2. To what extent are the four categories of self-esteem producing positive feelings of self-worth and value for each man?

3. Why are the salesmen discontented?

4. What do you think the presence of "show of interest" cards means?

5. How does each of the key people normally project his power? What styles are overused?

---

[1] Curbstoning comes in many forms; but it basically describes a situation where salesmen make private deals to the detriment of the dealership.

chapter eight

Power and conflict

Figure 8.1 summarizes the effective and less effective overuse of the six power styles. As you consider the diagram, think about the processes it suggests in terms of these questions:

1. When and under what conditions in the past have you used *each* major style?
2. Which style have you overused and under what conditions?
3. Who in your company or other organization seems to use each style most often?

One condition that is common in virtually every organization is conflict. It is probably inevitable, and by itself neither good nor bad. A great deal of conflict in organizations comes about precisely because of the different ways we seek to express our power to gain self-respect. Conflict that occurs during the everyday, normal uses of power can be productive, challenging, and even fun. This is true because people who approach situations from the three very different perspectives—personal, interpersonal, and

FIGURE 8.1.

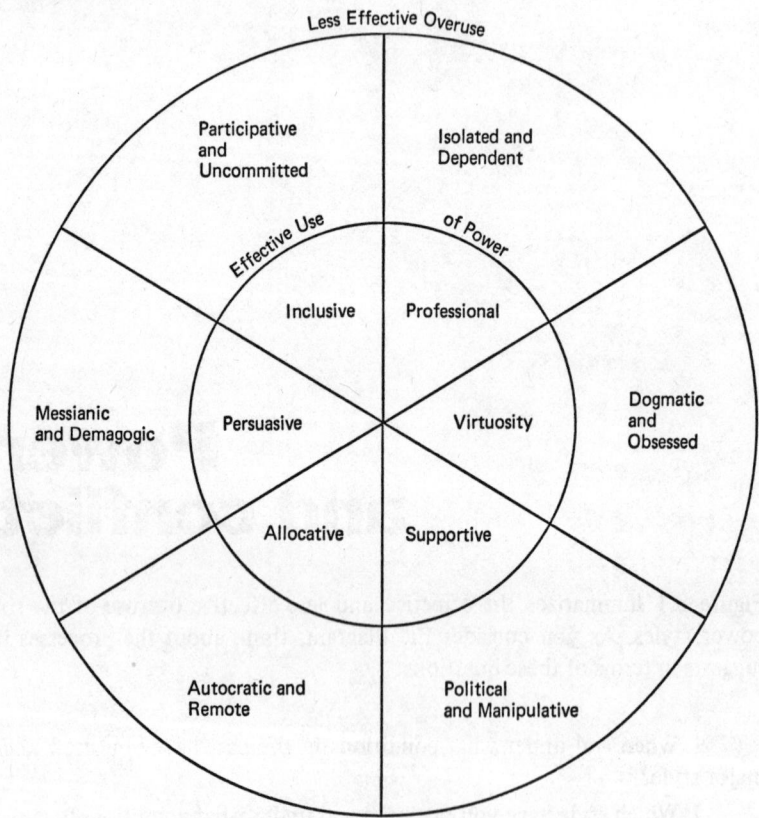

Inner circle (Effective Use of Power): Inclusive, Professional, Virtuosity, Supportive, Allocative, Persuasive

Outer circle (Less Effective Overuse): Participative and Uncommitted, Isolated and Dependent, Dogmatic and Obsessed, Political and Manipulative, Autocratic and Remote, Messianic and Demagogic

structural—can often provide each other with valuable insights and perspectives.

But when stress, fear, or opposition cause the frequent overuse of various power styles, conflict can quickly escalate to noisy confrontation. For example, if your preferred power approach is personal mastery, skill, and virtuosity, you may be very uncomfortable if your boss uses the formality and control of the allocation style. You may feel tied down by the structure, rules, and policies your boss relies on. Your boss, on the other hand, may be uncomfortable when you use the visionary, independent behaviors typical of the virtuoso style. He or she may see you as a troublemaker or even as disloyal.

Although you and your boss may not be really comfortable with each other, your two different approaches can be very helpful in dealing with a range of problems and opportunities. In your area of expertise, you may be able to provide novel solutions and approaches your boss hadn't considered, while he or she may provide the structure and resources required for accomplishment.

One of the more useful things peers, bosses, and subordinates can do together is to privately reflect on the ways they prefer to use power and then to openly share and talk about their preferences. In this way, we become better able to use our differences for productive, esteem-enhancing purposes.

When someone uses a power style quite different from yours, it may feel and appear strange or uncomfortable. It is easy to ascribe such differences to all sorts of unworthy motives in the other. Remember, however, that person is trying only to gain the same feelings of self-respect and self-worth we all seek and need.

The situation is quite different when a power style is overused. Things become even more tense and less productive when several people overuse their preferred approaches. Please refer to Figure 8.1. You will see that an organization is likely to have severe problems when several styles are overused or where any one approach is overused by several people. Ineffective as it is almost certain to be, this is exactly the situation in many organizations. The results are a significant decline in personal feelings of worth and value, and reduced individual and organization productivity.

Overuse of a power style results from lowered self-esteem, and it usually also causes a still greater reduction. When we overuse our preferred approach, we prevent ourselves from gaining self-esteem from one or more of the four sources. It may appear paradoxical, but overuse of a power style usually makes us less powerful. Moreover, overuse can reduce the likelihood both of real achievement and of being cared about by others.

When several managerial level people in an organization engage in the overuse of their preferred styles or when the most senior level executive frequently does so, we can predict decreased organizational vitality and performance. These are not easy conditions to overcome. Generally, a third party has to become involved. The third party's role will often be to try to determine the specific barriers to self-esteem that cause the power overuse. He or she will then help the parties renegotiate their roles and behaviors toward each other and may try to influence higher level executives to make any broader changes that are required. Usually, when the barriers to individual self-esteem are removed, the power overuse rapidly declines and the conflicts can be handled.

Effective supervisors and managers are often adept at handling such situations between their subordinates as neutral third parties. Sometimes, however, an outside third party will be more effective. Think back to your answers to the three questions on page 63. Have you identified some specific type of situation where you are more inclined to overuse one or another power approach? Try to describe for yourself the specific kinds of events that make you feel powerless and that lead to overusing your style. If you can do so, you will have made a strong start toward managing your self esteem through a more effective use of your influence. When you encounter similar situations, or believe you are likely to, there are some alternatives.

1. It may be possible to avoid, restructure, or postpone the potential trigger situation where you are likely to respond to frustration with an overuse of your style.

2. If possible, take time to reflect on the situation and select the style or styles that are most likely to get you what you want, and that will probably leave you feeling good about yourself.

3. Mentally rehearse the use of the styles you select. Who is likely to say what? How are you likely to feel in the situation? How can you gain or avoid losing self-esteem? How will you try to influence the course of events? This rehersal will often allow you to be far more effective and also to gain more positive feelings about yourself.

4. Is there any preparation you can do either alone, such as gathering information and viewpoints, or with someone else? For example, you might rehearse the approach you've selected with another, or you might seek to form a temporary, mutually supportive alliance with someone else who will be involved.

The purpose of these suggestions is to help you gain, or at least not lose, self-esteem in conditions that tend to be threatening or frustrating. Self-respect in such situations is most likely to be maintained when you deliberately select who you will seek to influence, what power styles you will use, and how you can avoid giving away your power through the overuse of any style.

POWER AND LOSS

There is another group of situations where most of us will feel basically powerless, ineffective, and at a loss about what to do. When these situations occur, our self-esteem plummets. These are experiences where we lose something or someone of enormous value and meaning to us. We are not faced with someone else's power overuse decreasing our own influence and hence ability to gain self-respect. Rather, temporarily overwhelming conditions make us feel depressed or angry because there appears nothing we can do to influence the situation.

Most of us have had such painful loss experiences as:

1. Death of a spouse or other close family member.
2. Divorce and/or separation.
3. Loss of our job.
4. Major financial reversals.
5. Personal injury or illness.
6. Retirement.

These events won't have the identical effect on everybody, but they surely represent painfully wounding situations for most of us. These are loss experiences. In each case, something once greatly valued and desired is taken away and is no longer available. Loss experiences are so hurtful because our self-esteem is hammered. The people, security, relationships, and identifications involved were valued so highly because they contributed very greatly to our sense of personal worth and value.

Each of these losses provided self-esteem from one or several of the four sources.

1. They allowed us to see our achievements.
2. They provided evidence that we were cared about and valued.
3. They allowed us to exercise some power and influence.
4. They were situations congruent with some deeply held values and beliefs.

We should not be surprised at the powerful emotions of sadness, grief, anger, depression, disorientation, and rage that such losses cause. We have literally lost something of ourselves, and our sense of self-worth and value. There are enormous stresses associated with such events. Chapter 14 considers some ways of dealing with stress and pressure.

Of all the four sources of self-esteem that may be eliminated or reduced by such losses, none is likely to be as important as the massive loss of our own ability to influence events. With each type of major loss, we feel basically helpless and ineffective. Esteem from one or another of the other sources may also be reduced, but the most massive impact is usually the way we feel about our ability to cause change and to have any influence over what has happened. We may feel useless, ineffective, and overwhelmed. And there seems to be nothing we can do about it. In some of the examples of loss, there is in fact nothing to be done.

The healing and recovery of our self-esteem will often take months or even longer if the loss has been a major one. A key element in this healing amounts to a process of detaching ourselves from what has been lost and eventually reattaching to other people, relationships, and situations. This detachment and reattachment is visible evidence that, once again, we have some power and some control. The feelings of improved self-esteem that accompany the effective use of our own influence, even after a major loss, point out an important lesson.

> The sooner and more effectively we can demonstrate to ourselves power, control, and influence, the more rapidly our self-respect and feelings of being strong, worthwhile, and competent will improve.

This seems to be true anytime our self-esteem is at a low point. It suggests that as soon as we are able, we should seek out ways to use our personal power. That use is the vehicle through which self-esteem from the other three sources will more rapidly become available. The result will be a more quickly reestablished sense of self-esteem and improved performance in many areas of our lives.

chapter nine

Some characteristics of personal power in organizations

Various writers have considered power from a sociological perspective. I believe power is primarily a basic, individual characteristic and a psychological concept. The concept of power is the same, however it is expressed. It amounts to causing others to do what we wish so as to gain self-esteem for ourselves. Power is expressed through institutions of some kind, whether they be a nation, office, church, or family. It requires others' involvement. As we have seen, it can be expressed in six quite different ways, and it can also be more, or less, effectively employed. But the concept is the same. It just looks and feels different in some situations than in others.

Power is a personal characteristic of individual people. Virtually everyone has exercised at least some of his or her own. To be sure, power is expressed in a social context, in groups as small as two people or as large as nations. But it is less a characteristic of groups or organizations than a desire and impulse of individual human beings who use organizations to gain, express, and extend their power beyond their immediate boundaries. To use groups for this purpose, the groups must have some organization and some structure for assigning, exercising and distributing power. As we have noted, organizations with a pyramidal design are dominant in Western society.

One's influence, effectively expressed privately, is typically aimed at achievement or accomplishment, which is one component of self-esteem. That same influence expressed *toward and through other people* is power. The exercise of personal power is really limited only by what an individual *can* do or by what he *wants* to do.

"Can do" factors include a complex of personal characteristics, knowledge, abilities, skills, and external restraints. "Want to do" factors are values, ethics, and belief systems that are at the core of another of the four components of self-esteem, as we saw in Figure 2.1., page 7.

These are limiting or direction-giving forces consisting of beliefs, ethics, and values. When we act in accord with our beliefs, we feel good about who we are: We gain self-esteem. For most of us, our personal notions of morality and ethics impose some restraints on the ways we gain, express, and extend our power. For some—fortunately few—internal restraints are largely absent. We see in the news every day stories about random violence, vandalism, and murder. The behavior of many of the leaders of Nazi Germany suggests the near absence, or breakdown, of those restraints on a large scale.

To consider a more positive example, the modern corporation is a place where power can be gained and exercised. Indeed, in many bureaucratic organizations accomplishment and achievement is not especially rewarded, but the acquisition of power is. It is probably true that those who achieve organizational levels that permit significant expression of personal power also share some basic values and beliefs. There is a striking consistency of belief among relatively senior power-wielders across many different kinds of organizations. This seems true even though such people rarely talk together about values. And, of course, most of them have never even met.

People who choose business as the arena to gain and exercise power generally share a belief in a free enterprise economic system, in the probability and essential rightness of rewards for diligent work, in organization loyalty, and in similar values. Those who gain significant positions in the organization usually share positive values about the particular organization's specific aims and activities as well as more general beliefs. Those who don't, usually leave, fail, or otherwise reduce their commitment to the organization.

The congruence of power with some sort of value system as suggested above highlights an important issue. In our experience with a large number of organizations, both profit and nonprofit, we have never encountered the effective use of power in the absence of some shared system of beliefs, values, and ethics. This does not mean that all details of such belief systems are necessarily and openly agreed on by all organization members, and it certainly does not mean that beliefs, ethics, and morality are regular matters for discussion. But in subtle ways, people do communicate their beliefs, values, ethics, and morality. Those in positions that permit and encourage the exercise of power generally share some important beliefs. When brought together in an open and protected environment such as an executive education program, the congruence and agreement about fundamental values is often extraordinary.

Power, as we have seen, is the driving force behind our efforts to gain self-esteem. Our values provide the direction for such efforts. Both are also key components of self-esteem. The critical role of values in achieving self-esteem remains an important and largely unexplored area of inquiry.

Members of many, perhaps most, organizations have a sense of "we-ness"; a shared sense of what the organization is all about. For the most part, organization members in reasonably powerful positions, such as management or technical specialties, tend to agree with the correctness of the organization's mission as they understand it. This seems especially true in line, sales, or operating organizations where the organization's purpose is generally clear. For example, it is usually much easier to identify the shared values in such organizations than in the corporate staffs of large conglomerates. Individual members can more readily see the values and beliefs inherent in line or operating organizations, can more readily influence the organization's actions, and can see visible and measurable results. Or, because the basic values can usually be inferred, individual members can decide how well the organization's values and their own match and decide to stay or leave.

Because of this relative value clarity and agreement, especially in smaller, line-type organizations, power is usually more effectively gained, expressed, and extended—and in more different ways. One predictable result is that people in such organizations usually have a greater sense of personal worth and value—of self-esteem—than people in equivalent, or even higher level, positions in corporate staff or support roles.

Except, perhaps, at the very top of a large bureaucratic organization, such as a major conglomerate, the basic values of the organization are often quite unclear until operating or line-level positions are reached. Because of this relative lack of value clarity, the sense of "we-ness" is often absent. Power in such situations tends to be ineffectively expressed—permitted power styles are few, and many members not only demonstrate, but also describe a low level of self-esteem. When we look at a variety of historical events, we see that power has most effectively been expressed in the presence of some articulated and reasonably agreed upon system of values and beliefs. This seems true however power is shown and demonstrated. In summary:

1. Power is intensely personal and individual in use. It is a personal, not just a social, phenomenon.

2. It is expressed in multiperson contexts; some sort of organization and structure is needed.

3. The typical bureaucratic organization distributes and allocates power largely through authority and the formal structure.

4. The effective use and expression of personal power is intimately bound up with and demonstrated through some core of ideas, beliefs, and values.

5. Such beliefs and values must be generally shared, and are in most successful organizations. Some level of agreement on fundamental values seems necessary for power to be distributed, accepted and assigned. When there is little value and belief clarity, power tends to be ineffectively expressed, and the self-esteem of organization members suffers.

chapter ten

Organization assumptions and personal power

In recent years many of the complaints against business organizations, educational and medical institutions, and government agencies have centered on the ways they are managed and administered. There seems to be a consensus that the way many of these institutions are organized is simply out of date. Absenteeism, turnover, and frequent job changes, together with antibusiness sentiments, reduced quality and quantity of output all testify to a general dissatisfaction with the way things are. A great many organizations permit power to be expressed *only* through the more remote, structural styles we have been considering. The predictable result is that many people have few opportunities to obtain positive feelings of self-worth and value on the job. Both they and the organization suffer.

This organizational challenge is faced by many institutions in what seems to be rapidly developing as a whole new set of requirements and expectations evolving from the period of bureaucracy we seem to be leaving behind. What this new era will become is not clear, but it seems sure to be very different from what we have experienced before. In government, business, medicine, education, religion, and justice traditional forms of organization are proving inadequate either to achieve organization performance, or to permit and foster individual self-esteem. Essentially, the times require a shift from a bureaucratic to a much more dynamic and participative approach; from a preoccupation with structure and authority to concern about how the organization goes about accomplishing its mission; from power based purely on formal position to influence expressed in a variety of ways.

As we have seen, there are several ways personal power can be expressed. People of all kinds are more often demanding an effective voice in matters affecting their lives. In doing so, they are challenging organizational principles and values that have long been traditional in modern Western civilization. Organized taxpayer revolts, coalitions of neighborhood, consumer, and environmental action groups, a growing underground or off-the-books economy estimated at over $2.5 billion, and other examples could be cited to show that many people are demanding the ability to use their own power and influence in their own ways.

Rapid change in nearly every aspect of business, together with the emerging demands of employees and managers, suggest that the way many organizations function is inadequate in important ways.

Briefly, the way organizations are structured and the way they function are products of a basic philosophy shared and generally accepted over a long period of time. Only now is that philosophy being questioned. The approach that seems to have dominated Western organizational style acts as if the universe is, essentially, a machine.

In this view, time is a straightforward, historical flow of events from the "first cause" through sequential cause-and-effect relationships, one after the other. This notion assumes that the cause-and-effect process is both linear and one way: A causes B, but B cannot cause A. Many senior managers act as if they believe their organizations work according to this linear, one way pattern. For example:

1. Department X is not producing up to its potential.
2. The department manager must be at fault (it is easier if we can find someone to blame).
3. If I replace the department manager,
4. Then the department will produce better.
5. So, I will replace the manager.

It may work out just as the senior manager hopes. But many times it does not. The organizational system usually doesn't behave according to a neat set of sequential cause-and-effect relationships. Fear, disruption of informal ways of getting things done, broken communication patterns, and many other things occur when the old manager is removed and a new one brought in. Sometimes such a change makes things worse.

Translating this kind of mechanical view into organizational terms is straightforward. If the universe is a machine, then it, like all machines, is designed on the basis of functional hierarchies in which each "higher" step in the structure controls those below. If you have ever looked into an old clock, you will see only one or a few wheels turning in response to the weights or springs. But you will see many smaller gears controlling the clock's actions as determined by movements of the larger wheels. That is an illustration of functional hierarchies. Social structures, it was felt, must also reflect this kind of organization. That is, they must be hierarchical, and each must have a controlling agent. As noted earlier, the family is headed by a father, the state by a king, the Catholic Church by a Pope, and the corporation by a president. By virtue of his position at the top of the hierarchy, each of these people is granted considerable power over his organization and control of its wealth. It took centuries for this view of organizations to become widely accepted, and there are many who will struggle to maintain such a structure. So we should not be surprised if the evolution and acceptance of new organization principles, forms, and processes takes time. But it seems clear that such evolution and acceptance are occurring at an increasing rate.

Against this philosophical backdrop, bureaucracy emerged as a dominant organizational style. Several authors have described what seem to be the major characteristics of a bureaucracy:

1. A clear and well-defined chain of command.
2. Rules, regulations, and procedures for dealing with work activities.
3. A division of labor based on specialization.
4. Rewards based on technical competence.
5. Impersonality in human relations.

This is a relatively remote or structural use of power: in our terms, allocation or professional. A bureaucracy is best pictured as a pyramid with authority, control, and power concentrated at its narrow peak and declining with each step down the hierarchy until, at the broad base, people are simply carrying out instructions. In sum, the bureaucratic organization is autocratic. A person's authority and power are derived largely from his position in the hierarchy. Planning and decision-making occur at the top and flow downward in a (presumed) one-way sequence of cause-and-effect. Power in a great many organizations is permitted to be expressed only through the allocation or professional modes. The result is that many employees at nearly all organization levels are unable to use their own power styles to obtain self-esteem in the context of their work. A predictable result has been the decline in productivity and innovation so widely noted in recent years.

Authority has remained largely a function of position so that a bureaucratic style has been, essentially, self-perpetuating. Those in powerful positions have maintained the past in the name of "stability", the "long-range", or even the "social order". They have trained young people and younger members of the organization to adapt and adjust to the demands of stability. Rules, policies, and laws have been formulated (and enforced) which have both enshrined stability and strengthened the bureaucratic management system.

It would be easy to challenge the bureaucratic system on grounds that it is autocratic, static, and based on a mechanical view of man as, indeed, it is. But the fact is that authoritarian, pyramidal organizations have been remarkably efficient, particularly in the production of goods and services. They have created much wealth and fostered great technical advancement. Ironically, it is these very accomplishments that are making bureaucracy passé. The affluence and expectations of a majority of Americans have produced new attitudes and expectations among employees and their children. Moreover, the relatively recent notion that organizational and psychological phenomena can usefully be thought of as the actions of systems rather than just sequential cause/effect chains has produced considerable change in our ideas about man and his organization.

The possibility and necessity of a systems approach became apparent only recently. Its necessity resulted from the fact that a mechanical scheme of isolated, causal chains of separate events simply can't deal with the challenges and problems faced by modern organizations. The organization of a system is simple *if* the system is only a serial or additive chain of components, each of which is understood. But as soon as this straight line addition is exceeded, an organized system rapidly becomes much more complex. At the other extreme of complexity (and most human organizations approach this point), the number of entities, events, or factors is so large that the interactions can be described only in probabilities. That is, we can usually only say that if this event happens, and if that event happens, there is a certain likelihood of a particular outcome. In human organizations, neat linearity is largely absent.

A good many authors, among them the late Abraham Maslow, have described the characteristics of what have variously been called fulfilled, meta-motivated, or self-actualized people. Such people are described as devoted to their work and as valuing meaningful tasks more than they value their wages alone. They actively seek positions of responsibility and consider freedom more desirable than simple security. This is a view quite different from earlier mechanistic views of man as seeking only an equilibrium condition or reduction of tension as described by proponents of classical psychoanalysis and learning theory. As the post-industrial era unfolds, the number of meta-motivated people is rapidly growing.

Changes in the basic interests, attitudes and expectations of employees have been studied, researched, and reported by many others. Various writers and researchers have depicted the emerging worker as one who "declines to be bored," who often would rather quit than be enslaved by unchallenging routine. Considerable research has showed that many of today's employees take it for granted that their jobs will provide adequate wages and fringe benefits, enlightened management, and good human relationships. These expectations seem to have a continuity despite ups and downs in the economy. Beyond these basics, however, many employees demand that their jobs fulfill their need for self-esteem. Interestingly, even workers laid off from their jobs maintain their notions of accomplishment. They hope to have some influence in matters of importance to them, they expect to see moral and ethical behavior from their employers and supervisors, and they want evidence of being cared about and valued as unique, worthwhile individuals. These are intense personal needs. They demonstrate far more than a linear, equilibrium seeking view of human nature.

There is considerable evidence that steadily increasing numbers of people are moving well beyond survival and security toward demands for opportunities to gain greater self-esteem. The past effectiveness of bureaucratic organizations in creating wealth and technology has, I believe, been largely responsible for this change. For example, we have the situation, once almost inconceivable, of union members bargaining not just for wages but for more *fulfilling jobs,* for *freedom* to reject overtime work, for some influence over working conditions, and the like. Now, new kinds of organizations must be created to aid fulfillment of positive feelings of personal worth and value. This task was difficult and singularly important in times of plenty, power, and productivity. Today it is essential.

As this book is written, much of the world is in the midst of considerable economic uncertainty. Unemployment in the United States stands over 10 percent and some basic industries such as construction and auto manufacturing are greatly depressed. Still, many technology companies and service businesses are growing rapidly. The face of "smokestack mid-America" is changing, as many people seek new opportunities, new careers, and new lives in different industries and different regions. They are taking responsibility for themselves, trusting neither business, nor unions nor the government. Most will, of course, find no pot of gold, but they *have* deliberately exercised their personal power. To that extent, they have improved or regained a sense of personal worth and self-respect.

However, in such an economic climate, some of the demands for autonomy, personal power, and fulfilling work are muted. The desires remain, but for many the focus is now more on security and safety. We can expect recovery to be accompanied by renewed demands for more personal influence and power. Indeed, such desires seem to become more pointed and more specific with each succeeding economic cycle.

It seems to me that a central, though rarely recognized, issue for many people in most organizations is that of the real extent of their personal power both over events and their own lives. Most of us have far more power than we use. In this post industrial period, increasing numbers of people are demanding power. Unlike their parents, many are unwilling to grant the legitimacy of relatively absolute organization power. Essentially, people are demanding that the organization spread its power throughout the hierarchy rather than hoard it only at the top. With increasing frequency, employees at all levels seem to be saying to their organizations, "Look, I'm a worthwhile, effective person. Treat me as one."

These powerful needs for self-esteem are so strong that powerlessness is simply unacceptable to many. Many people are increasingly resentful when they feel manipulated by remote authority and controlled as though they are so many interchangeable parts. You or someone you know probably knows the feeling of being told to clean out your desk and go because you don't seem to fit, aren't loyal, or offended someone important. You felt manipulated. You were. And you resent it deeply because being manipulated by others is clear evidence that one has *no* personal power in the situation.

Further, the emergence of these needs to use and express one's personal power to gain self-esteem may explain why anything less than *real* participation and *meaningful* involvement has not succeeded. Pseudo-human relations tactics are quickly noticed and rapidly discounted. Deliberately false approaches fail because they depend on the organization retaining relatively absolute power over its members. For example, the top executive of one corporation said recently, "We want our people to *feel* involved and that we value their ideas." But virtually every decision made in that corporation is made by a very few top level executives. In nearly every department, the decisions are made and rules enforced only by the department head. The allocation style dominates.

In short, the work ethic, the profit motive, and needs for security that provided ample incentive during the industrial age are simply not enough for many people today. Growing numbers of people are concerned with other factors: the quality of life, the challenge of the job, and the satisfaction of doing it well. The effect of much organizational behavior, however, is to prevent visible, personally important achievement, and accomplishment on the job.

Considerable evidence strongly suggests that the achievement motive is learned, and that the achievement motive can be taught and learned by individuals and whole communities. A great many organizations limit this learning and its expression in the organizational context. There is some evidence that the need for achievement has been declining in the United States for the past thirty years or so. I suspect the dominance of modern bureaucratic organizations is a major reason. If parents are not allowed to gain self-esteem through achievement, or through the expression of personal power and influence in a large part of their daily lives, they will be less likely to teach behavior such as early self-reliance, risk-taking, and risk assessment to their children.

Moreover, the top-down impersonality in human relationships so typical of bureaucratic systems is resented by increasing numbers of people who are demanding more caring relationships. This, of course, is one of the four components of self-esteem. Bureaucracy, with its rigid hierarchy and its one-way flow of authority, is ill-suited to providing opportunities for self-esteem through personally important achievement or genuinely caring relationships. Moreover, only relatively few of the organization's members have the opportunity to gain self-esteem by expressing their own power and influence. It is, finally, true that the ethical issues faced by many organizations are out of reach (though not out of awareness) for most members.

In our consulting practice we are also increasingly finding employees of client organizations who describe management or executive actions they feel to be immoral or unethical. Most often these employees feel basically powerless to improve the situation. They feel badly about themselves for remaining members of such an organization. Some seek other employment, but many others just put in their required time. In important ways they, too, have left the organization.

A new *kind* of organization is required—one which will emphasize process rather than solely structure, and substitute increased free human interaction for the impersonal chain of command. What is emerging is a recognition that new concepts, new ideas, and new categories are required and that self-esteem is central to both satisfaction and performance. These ideas, in one way or another, are all centered about the notion of "system."

Important systems, or models, seem to have periods of ebb and flow. They have periods of great success and periods of obsolescence. For a time, each is seen as a triumph, but later it may be viewed as an obstruction. The bureaucratic organization may have outlived its triumphs. A new style of organizing for human endeavor is emerging, and its roots lie in system theory.

Human life is not mechanical, not dependent upon simple cause-and-effect relationships or sequential addition, and it is not entirely rational. Instead, it is organic and fluid, dependent upon interpersonal and intergroup relations, and intuitive, embracing not only intellect but emotions and feelings.

What has happened is that remarkably similar ideas and principles have evolved in the enormously varied disciplines of modern science. In the past, science often tried to explain observable events by reducing them to an interplay of elementary units (that is, atoms, conditioned reflexes, traits, and so on) which could be studied independently of each other. We have all seen similar approaches used in business organizations where the emphasis is almost solely on very discreet, short-term, easily measured and analyzed results. Managers and executives sometimes become so concerned with short-range, isolated indices that the organization's long-term performance is jeopardized. This short-term outlook has often been unfavorably compared with the much longer range systems approach taken by managers in some other nations and in other U.S. industries.

Now, ideas are appearing that are concerned with problems of wholeness and organization, and with dynamic interactions shown in the different behaviors of parts in a larger configuration. Issues of this nature have been appearing in all disciplines of science, whether inanimate things, living organisms, or social phenomena are involved. This correspondence is even more striking because the developments in the various disciplines were (and are) largely independent of each other, and based on different facts, techniques, and philosophies. However, there appear to exist some general laws which apply to any system of a certain type regardless of the elements involved. It is these laws or principles which make up system theory.

chapter eleven

Some principles

This chapter introduces some ideas most of us probably don't think about very often. If you reflect for a few moments on each idea, its application to the structure and function of human organizations will become clear. You might pick an organization you know well and think about how each of the principles below fits that organization, its behavior, and its history.

    One large area of system theory is the part that deals with *open* systems. Conventional physics, by contrast, deals with *closed* systems—systems considered to be isolated from their environment. Physical chemistry, as another example, deals with (among other events) reaction rates and chemical equilibria eventually established in a closed container where a number of chemicals are brought together. But many systems are not closed. Every living organism and every human organization is essentially an open system. They maintain themselves in a continuous inflow and outflow, and a building up and breaking down of components. A living system is never really in a state of equilibrium with everything in balance. Rather, living systems approach or maintain a so-called "steady state" as distinct from equilibrium. Open systems have many transactions and communications with their environments as they import and export energy and a variety of ideas, information, and substances.

Consider a battery and an automobile engine. In a battery, the chemical reaction produces electricity. The battery uses up its own components to produce the capacity for work in the form of electricity. Ultimately, the components are used up and the battery dies. We can get no further work from it. Now think about your car's engine. It requires fuel from the environment and puts back into the environment a variety of substances. Indeed it *must* do so if any work is to be obtained from it. So long as this set of transactions with the environment goes on, the engine will operate until it wears out. The battery is largely a closed system while the car engine is more like an open system. Human beings and their organizations are open systems.

A closed chemical system *must* eventually reach a state of equilibrium. A closed system in equilibrium does not need energy for its preservation, nor can we get energy from it. In order to do work, it is necessary that the system *not* be in a state of equilibrium. Continuous working potential is possible only in an open system. The apparent equilibrium found in a living organism is not a true equilibrium. It is a dynamic steady state, maintained at a certain distance from true equilibrium. Thus, it is capable of performing work, but it also requires a continuous input of energy.

As another analogy, think about what happens when you repeatedly wring out a dirty mop in a pail of water. Eventually the water in the mop and the water in the pail are equally dirty. You cannot clean the mop nor can you effectively clean the floor. In that sense, work is no longer possible from this largely closed system. But if you wring out your dirty mop in a sink with a drain and a supply of clean water entering the system, your mop can be cleaned and is capable of almost continuously performing work. This more open system can continue to do work—it has input and output transactions with the environment.

In the closed system, when the pail water and water in the mop become equally dirty there is equilibrium and no work is possible. In the sink example of an open system, there is no equilibrium and work is possible. The flow of clean water from the tap, to the sink, through the mop, and down the drain maintains a difference in the concentrations of dirt on the floor and in the mop. This steady state condition permits work to be done. The regularly refreshed mop can absorb dirt from the floor.

Systems theory deals with both open and closed systems and the many gradations between. Human beings and their organizations are open systems, transacting with their environment, capable of nearly endless refreshment and of doing work, and decidedly *not* in a state of equilibrium.

Man, as an *open system*, seeks more than just tension reduction or equilibrium. Rather, we are "wanting animals" who will go to considerable lengths to avoid equilibrium. Biologically and psychologically, life is not maintenance or restoration of equilibria, but is essentially maintenance of disequilibria, those steady states we have considered. Behavior not only tends to *release* tensions but also to *build up* tensions. Juvenile delinquents who commit crimes for fun, a new psychopathology resulting from too much leisure, the burgeoning population of mental hospitals, industrial sabotage on the production line, frequent job changes, and malignant boredom are all evidence that the notions of adjustment, conformity, and psychological and social equilibrium don't work. They don't work because man and his institutions are open, not closed, systems.

EQUIFINALITY

The system idea is a significant change in the way we typically think about individuals and organizations. Neither individuals nor organizations are simply linear sequences of added characteristics. Rather, both are composed of tremendous numbers of characteristics, events, perceptions, and values in a high degree of interaction through many loops of information flow. Both are best described in probabilistic terms. Event A *may* cause event B, but B *may* cause A, or something else *may* cause both A and B.

Considerable work in physics and other fields has led to important findings and to important general conditions. For example, there is the notion of *equifinality*, which has a counterpart in human organizations. In any closed system the final state is fully and completely determined by the initial conditions. The mop and pail water will ultimately become equally dirty. If either the initial conditions or the process is changed, the final state will also be changed. This is not true of open systems where the same final state may be reached from different initial conditions and in different ways.

Many human organizations are managed as if they are closed systems by those in top positions. Those managers are more and more often surprised, concerned, and angry when the organizational system behaves differently than they anticipate. The error lies in considering the organization and its individual members as closed systems whose behavior should be fully determined by the initial conditions—the resources supplied the organization, its structure, charter, leadership, and so on.

One senior executive expressed his sense of frustration, hurt and anger when more than 60 percent of his employees signed union "show of interest" cards. He was completely surprised, yet the activity had been going on for weeks if not months.

> I gave them every damn thing they could want. We have a nice cafeteria, steady work, and the best equipment. Why would they do this to me? Why didn't I *know* they were unhappy?

Notice the linear thinking. If I do A, B, and C, then employees will be productive and contented. Notice, too, the absence of any consideration of employee self-esteem from relationships, achievement, basic values or the use of personal power. We have repeatedly found that when people feel a lack of personal power through an inability to influence other people and events, they will act to gain some self-esteem. Power becomes the energizer with self-esteem the goal. They leave marriages, find a new employer, invest their energies in some nonwork activity, or they may join unions.

FEEDBACK

Combining characteristics of open systems with the idea of *feedback*, another important principle, permits a very different view of organization than that shown by most institutions. Feedback permits the maintenance of a steady state, not equilibrium. It is the seeking of a goal by monitoring deviations and progress into circular causal chains and mechanisms. A great many biological events fit this feedback model. For example, consider how our body temperature is maintained. Data about the system and its operation are drawn off and cycled back into an earlier stage of the process so as to modify what the system does. So our bodies stay about the same temperature despite wide differences in the temperature of the air around us. Our body temperature is maintained at a steady state around 98° F. But it is not maintained in equilibrium. If it were, our temperature would be the same as that of our environment.

Consider the thermostat. When it is set at some predetermined point, it controls furnace operation and, hence, temperature within a few degrees. As the temperature increases, the thermostat "senses" the increase and, when the temperature is near the predetermined level, signals the furnace to "stop." In auto racing, the pit crew will regularly monitor information such as lap times, their driver's position in the field of racers, track conditions, and so on. They often communicate such data to their driver by using large sign boards he can see as he speeds by. The driver adds this information to what *he* knows about the car's condition and handling, and modifies and adjusts his behavior toward the goal of winning the race.

In the example on page 86, the executive was surprised, hurt and angry when his employees expressed interest in a union. He was surprised and said, "Why didn't I *know* they were unhappy?" Yet, there was ample evidence of employee dissatisfaction. Turnover and absenteeism were high, and productivity was not what it should have been with the new equipment.

Somehow, the feedback process broke down. Maybe the information never reached the executive. Or maybe he didn't *want* to hear the information. So he continued to manage the organization as if it was a closed rather than open system. He ignored, or at least did not seek out, available information.

GROWTH

A third characteristic of open systems is that they show *stepwise growth behavior and growth plateaus*. In other words, having passed some critical state, the system starts off on a new way of behaving. The system shows adaptive behavior by trial and error or experimentation. It tries new behaviors and eventually settles down so that it no longer conflicts with key elements of its environment. The process looks like a stair step with plateaus, sudden changes, and a higher plateau.

A child mastering the spoon or a monkey figuring out how to join poles together to reach a hanging banana are examples of step function behavior. First, there is a period of experimentation, then a sudden increase in available knowledge, followed by a period when the organism uses what it has learned—the child feeds itself. And the cycle begins again with more trial and error.

Entire societies have displayed this principle throughout their existence. The invention of the steam engine, for example, radically altered the lives of many who eventually learned to use the new knowledge to obtain something more from their environment. Recent innovations in electronics are sure to have profound implications for all of us.

Business (and other) organizations often display striking examples of step function behavior. Consider the entrepreneur who, together with a few like-minded friends, creates a new business. The business prospers, new employees join the company and quite suddenly the entrepreneur is faced with significant managerial problems. He can no longer control every significant behavior of the organization. So, he experiments with adding levels in the hierarchy or establishing particular functions, thereby placing himself still further from the individual employees. But he does have time to indulge in more entrepreneurial activity. At this point, the organization is quite different than it originally was. Organizations usually show a series of trial-and-error experiments over their existence. Closed systems do not show this sort of adaptive experimentation.

Individuals and organizations, too, show spurts of growth and also attain plateaus when little change is evident. During a plateau period significant change in behavior may not even be possible. We are most often consulted by new clients when they sense their organization is nearing a time of rapid change, or when they sense that it must change to survive or capitalize on major opportunities. For example, we have regularly observed that single location organizations experience these spurts at about five employees, again around a staff size of fifteen, again at forty-five to fifty, and again at a size of between ninety and one hundred employees. Indeed, we have seen similar regularity in larger organizations. For some reason these seem to be major hurdles for organizations—they will either stay much as they are and perhaps decline, or will become significantly different.

Anticipating and managing these stages of organization growth is not easy. The process is not easy, either, at an individual level as any parent can attest. The key to a successful organization transition from one plateau to another lies in providing opportunities for the unique, individual expression of personal influence by as many of those concerned as possible. Through these opportunities, organization members gain an improved sense of self-esteem and personal value.

chapter twelve

Individuals as systems

As living entities, we must interact with our environments. At a basic level we must take in oxygen, food, and water to live. We put back into the environment a variety of chemical compounds that are waste to us but useful to other living systems. As open systems, we constantly interact with other systems and cannot exist otherwise.

We show characteristics of both open and closed systems. That is, our behavior is often exploratory, resulting in sudden increases in skills or knowledge and growth plateaus. We find a wide range of ways of supporting our families, obtaining an education, or accomplishing other objectives (equifinality) and we constantly obtain and use data about our own behaviors as seen by others or as compared against some standard (feedback). Much of what it means to be human comes about precisely because we *are* open systems.

All of us show a mixture of open and closed system behaviors. In most of our lives we act very much like an open system. In other areas of our lives we are restrained, or often restrain ourselves, and are held to a restricted position more characteristic of a closed system. Within the limits of our genetic possibilities, we are perhaps the most open systems around.

The problem is that through childhood experiences and training, the actions of the rigid educational system, and the behaviors of the largely bureaucratic organizations where we earn our livings, we often begin to act like closed systems.

Experimental actions leading to possible, step-wise growth often tend to become greatly restricted over what they can be and, indeed, frequently were as a child. Many of us increasingly tend to perceive and act as if only a very limited range of actions will help achieve some objective, and we increasingly avoid or ignore feedback data about our own behavior. Because we are largely open systems, these changes are not inherent to our natures. They are learned behaviors enforced by societal institutions that have control over rewards and punishments in the allocation power style.

So long as rewards were scarce, as they have been for most of man's existence, this molding and shaping of individual behavior by institutions was acceptable to most people, and the bureaucratic organization *was* effective in meeting the most basic human needs. The increasing rate of change, together with far more widely available ways of meeting our needs has changed all that. As basic survival needs have been met, as governmental programs—Social Security, welfare, educational loans, and so on—have been implemented to provide increased predictability and security, and as population growth and travel have provided increased opportunities for social interaction, a whole new order of motivations and drives have come into play. These motivations center around self-esteem.

Most bureaucratic organizations depend on an allocation power style and rely on the control of formal rewards and punishments. This use of power was generally acceptable when formal rewards were rare. If by rewards we mean only money or its organizational equivalents, rewards do remain limited. But today many employees sense that *other kinds* of rewards exist. Opportunities for increased self-esteem and, especially, permission to use one's power and influence are possible in most organizations when they are allowed to operate more as open systems. It appears that a large and growing number of people are motivated by desires to contribute meaningfully in individual ways and to obtain recognition for this effort and contribution. Increasingly, freedom to experiment, to have a significant voice in matters affecting one's world, including conditions of work, satisfying interpersonal relationships, and interesting work content, are being demanded.

In a very loose way we can say that because most organizations are often managed as closed systems, there is little recognition that the organization can reach its goals in a great many different ways. It can look and behave very differently than the usual bureaucratic structure or what it has historically been. And yet, it can effectively meet objectives set for it. Indeed, it will often do so informally anyway because it *is* largely an open system despite the consternation of managers who are discomfited by the organization (and its individual members) not behaving "the way we do things around here," or "according to the rules." Since an organization is largely an open system, it contains numerous feedback loops, many of which are regularly ignored, and other loops can be deliberately built-in. There is, or can be, a constant flow of information back into the system. Processes can be designed so that members of the organization constantly investigate alternative ways of "getting there from here," mutually set goals and objectives, and monitor feedback data of all sorts on a relatively immediate basis. Members, individually and through their organizations, can deliberately adopt trial-and-error behavior in a new situation before a final decision is made, monitor the results through feedback mechanisms, and plan for the time when, as in a growth step, the organization's size, objectives, markets, mission, and so on are different. These observations and analogies are not meant to be anthropomorphic. Although, as we've seen, organizations have many characteristics of open systems, they are not living organisms. They are the creations of senior managers, owners, and executives whose goals and desires are expressed by and pursued through the organization.

These three principles of growth, feedback, and equifinality, and others, *do* operate in organizations precisely because they are largely open systems. Management's choice is whether to try to ignore these system characteristics or to use them creatively and deliberately. Note that the three characteristics of open systems are far more concerned with *process* than with formal authority and structure alone. An open organization system can recognize, permit, and effectively use a variety of expressions of personal power and influence by its members. This will result in greater self-esteem for individuals and better performance by the organization.

There are many reasons, then, to be willing to sometimes modify the authoritarian pyramid and use, in addition, a more dynamic organizational form featuring give-and-take relationships among segments of a system and between whole systems, which combine to form still larger ones. Feedback, the two-way relationship among and between organizational units and people, is a key operating principle. If feedback occurs both within the organization and between it and other organizations, the system is open and organic.

Although an authoritarian bureaucracy can be very effective over short periods of time, the absence of feedback to the controlling group or person will often lead to ultimate failure. A good many organization managers ignore feedback, or at least don't seek it, and are much less effective than they might be. We need only reflect on Watergate to make the point. In that situation key White House staff members ignored, or at least avoided, widely available feedback from many sources. They progressively isolated themselves and ultimately lost their power to influence events. In contrast, an open system encouraging full interaction among all its internal parts and external environments, has the resources for regular self-renewal. The fundamental problem is that many institutions permit one's personal power and influence to be exhibited *only* in formal and structural ways. There are, however, functional groups in many organizations that allow employees and managers to regularly use other power styles. For example, many salespeople very successfully use a persuasive approach while scientists and engineers in research and development departments frequently prefer the virtuoso style. Often, problem-solving or project teams are directed by managers who tend to use an inclusive way of projecting their influence. But for most employees, there are few opportunities to have much influence, and the modes of expressing their power are similarly restricted. Those who typically project their influence other than through a formal allocation or professional approach are often actually disempowered. Moreover, usually only those at higher levels are enabled to express their power in even these limited ways. The result is a reduction in self-esteem for many individuals and decreased vitality for the organization.

The structure and authority styles so characteristic of many organizations *force* the organization and its members to behave in ways more typical of closed than open systems. People in many organizations simply feel unable to express their influence. That source of esteem is reserved largely for those near the top of the pyramid.

The power and esteem models described in this book and observations of many companies would suggest that of the four sources of self-esteem, the ability to have influence over people, situations, and events would be seen as the least available in most organizations. That is, we would expect employees at all levels to obtain less self-esteem from being able to have influence than from the remaining three sources.

The models would also suggest that self-esteem from the four sources would increase with successively higher level positions in the organization structure. Some recent research suggests that both predictions

TABLE 12.1 Rankings of Self-Esteem Received from the Four Sources by Employees in Six Companies

COMPANY:	Data processing service organization A	Oil company offices B	Computer software development company C	Foundry D	Large electrical products manufacturing plant E	Aerospace manufacturing plant F	All
ESTEEM SOURCE:							
Achievement and Accomplishment	1	1	1	1	1	1	1
Being valued and cared about	3	2	2	3	2	2	2
Ethical and moral behavior	2	3	3	4	3	3	3
Personal power and influence	4	4	4	2	4	4	4

NOTE: A low score means a relatively high level of satisfaction.

are probably accurate. Many organizations use confidential surveys and questionnaires that ask employees at all levels to describe and evaluate important aspects of their work environment. The specific questions asked depend on the needs of the particular organization, but our recent studies have also included items about each of the four sources of self-esteem. These questions ask organization members to describe the degree to which they feel satisfied about their experiences with each of the four sources of self-esteem. So far, more than 4,000 people from these organizations have responded to the self-esteem items. They represent business organizations as diverse as data processing services and foundries. The rankings of satisfaction with esteem from each source are given below: A rank score of *one* represents the highest level of satisfaction, a score of *four* is the lowest.

As we later learned, employees in the foundry were feeling badly about themselves and their organization because of a considerable number of unethical and even illegal managerial actions that were well-known. This probably explains the rank order difference in Company D. But in general, it seems true that employees obtain less self-esteem from expression of their own influence than from the remaining sources of esteem.

For managers and supervisors, the rankings were these:

TABLE 12.2 Rankings of Self-Esteem Received from the Four Sources by Managers and Supervisors in Six Companies

COMPANY:	A	B	C	D	E	F
Achievement	1	1.5	2	1	1	1
Cared About	2	1.5	3.5	3	2	2
Ethics	3	3	1	4	3	3
Power	4	4	3.5	2	4	4

NOTE: Achievement and being cared about were scored equally in Company B, while being cared about and personal power were scored the same in Company C.

The supervisory group in the foundry angrily told us of many occasions when they were told by top management to ship clearly defective products, not to perform contractually required tests, and other ethically questionable practices. Perhaps these situations explain the low order of self-esteem they receive from this source.

It generally seems that supervisors also receive less esteem from the expression of their personal influence than from the other sources. This condition is a predictable result of the closed nature of many organizations.

Our second expectation was that employees higher in the organization's structure would experience greater self-esteem than those at lower levels. Higher level people are usually allowed to use and project more of their personal influence. The relative level of self-esteem for various employee groups is shown below. In every case, the higher the job level the higher the amount of self-esteem experienced. The problem is that there are many more people at the bottom of the typical pyramid than there are at the middle or top.

In summary, we can say that a great many organizations use an allocation style and bureaucratic structure. Among the characteristics of such organizations are a top-down, remote power style, influence largely based on level in the hierarchy, impersonal relationships, and an adherence to formal structure and authority. These organizations are managed as though they are closed rather than open systems. Far more attention is given to structure than to process, and feedback about the organization's functioning is rejected, ignored, or denied. Options, alternatives, and choices are largely restricted to those permitted or initiated by authority figures.

Because people in the organization are restricted in the ways they can use their own power and because authority depends on a person's level in the hierarchy, we would expect to find that employees feel relatively powerless. Further, we would anticipate that the amount of self-esteem would be lowest for those lower in the hierarchy and greater for those with higher level positions. As we have seen, both of these expectations appear to be the case.

Allowing more people to have some power and influence at work will increase positive feelings of personal value. Organization performance and individual self-esteem will both improve under such conditions. To accomplish this, new organization forms and new managerial perceptions are needed so that a variety of styles of personal influence are permitted and encouraged. Moreover, more influence and power must also be allowed those lower in the hierarchy. By allowing a broader range of personal power styles at all organization levels and by encouraging influence by those lower in the structure, self-esteem will increase for a large proportion of the organization's members. By attending to individual needs to express and project personal power, the organization will begin to operate more like the open system it inherently is. Improved organization perfor-

Table 12.3 Total Self-Esteem Received by Different Levels of Employees in Six Firms

COMPANY Employee Group:	A	B	C	D	E	F
Workers	Low	Low	Low	Low	Low	Medium
Supervisors	Medium					
Supervisors and Managers as a Group		High	Medium	Medium	Medium	Medium
Directors and Other Senior Managers	High		High	High	High	

mance will typically be very evident in a year to eighteen months, although many signs of improvement will be visible much earlier than that.

The 1980s likely will be characterized as an era of taking control. We will see a steady increase in efforts by individuals and relatively small groups to express significantly greater influence and power. There will be less dependence on, and more resistance to, remote, bureaucratic power.

Powerlessness is becoming increasingly unacceptable to many people in both their personal and work lives. We see evidence of this in:

1. A growing off-the-books, underground economy.
2. The rise of barter groups.
3. Taxpayer revolts.
4. Strikingly varied life styles.
5. A high divorce rate.
6. Steady decline in union membership and increasingly successful union decertification efforts.
7. Progressive growth of powerful, single interest citizen groups with influence at local, state, and federal levels.
8. High employee turnover, absenteeism, declining productivity.

You can probably add many more examples. The point is that many people are seeking and expressing their personal power in their own ways in many aspects of their lives. They are doing so to gain or regain a sense of personal efficacy and self-esteem.

chapter thirteen

A case study

As we have seen, power is as complex as the organizations in which it is expressed. But it is only by examining an organization that we can see how power really operates, how we might empower more employees, and the likely results of such actions. The study questions below will help you consider the following case studies.

STUDY QUESTIONS

1. How would you describe the self-esteem of employees, supervisors, and managers? Which of the four sources of esteem seem to be contributing least to employee feelings of personal worth and value?

2. What specific power styles do you suspect are operating in each of the departments and plants? Are any styles overused? How would you characterize the power styles used between the organization described and the parent company?

3. What are the organizational effects of the conditions and issues you have analyzed in response to questions 1. and 2. above?

4. How do you analyze the situation in terms of the characteristics of open systems we considered earlier?

A few years ago a large producer and marketer of soft drinks purchased a multiplant beverage franchise in a major and growing metropolitan center from its founder. The founder had actively operated the business, and he remained on site for some time after the acquisition and appointment of a new general manager. Market analyses clearly showed that the volume and profit potentials of the concern were both large and relatively untapped. Competition was generally weak; plant equipment and the truck fleet were in excellent condition. The newly acquired operation seemed poised for very significant gains. But the gains failed to materialize; sales and profits remained essentially flat during the first year with only modest improvement.

Executives from the parent company began to believe that managerial and organization weaknesses were inhibiting the capacity of the acquired company to capitalize on its opportunites. At the time of acquisition, the organization structure looked like Figure 13.1.

Altogether, the operation employed about 400 workers in three locations. The primary location was by far the largest. The organizational improvement effort began with a number of interviews, group discussions, observations, and a study of available records. Excerpts from the report covering these early impressions are summarized below and convey the feeling and tone of the company as we experienced it.

PRELIMINARY ORGANIZATION ASSESSMENT

Introduction

This recent acquisition was and is one of the largest beverage franchises in the country with well over 100 routes, more than 10,000 vending machines, and nearly 400 employees.

Eight man-days were required for numerous, detailed interviews in the three locations. All interviews were conducted in private, and confidentiality was assured. In addition, a large number of systematic observations of organization and individual behavior patterns were studied and analyzed as were some existing business records and reports.

FIGURE 13.1.

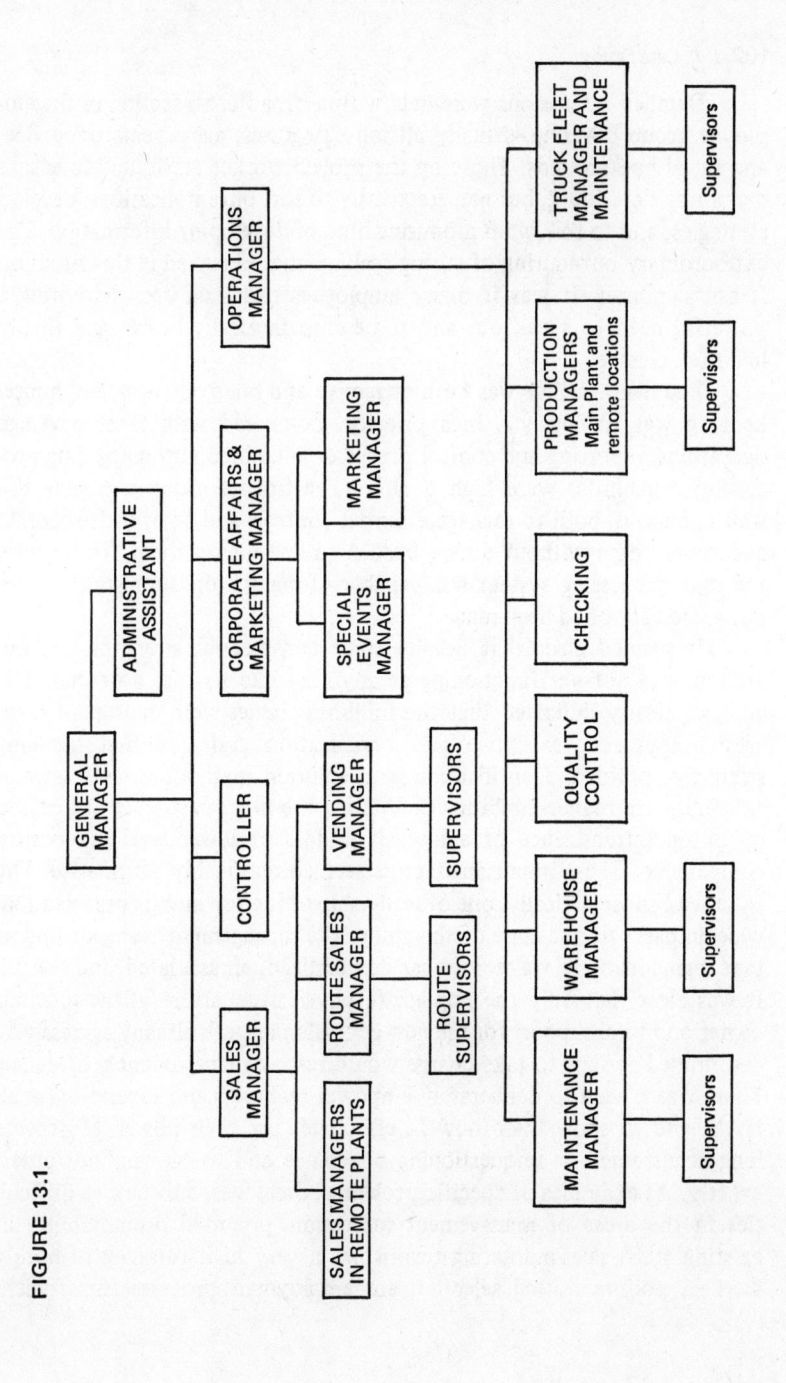

Detailed discussions were held with a broad cross section of the employee group covering virtually all job categories, ages, years of service, and racial backgrounds. Those on the project worked separately to ensure maximum data input, but met frequently to sort out implications, develop strategies, and to follow up promising lines of developing information. The extraordinary outpouring of strong feelings that occurred in this situation is not common. It was if many employees had long been harboring a powerful need to speak out and to be empathetically heard—and finally had their chance.

The main facility was both attractive and relatively new, and housekeeping was obviously a high priority. Compared with most beverage operations, reporting and control processes and allied automatic data processing capabilities were high quality. The finance group was generally well organized, both to manage essential controls and to provide accurate and timely data without undue burden to line management. To be sure, the data processing system was capable of many more sophisticated uses, but a good start had been made.

It seemed clear that despite some conspicuous strengths, the operation was not yet functioning at anything like its real potential. The analysis clearly indicated that the inhibiting issues were matters of managerial approach, executive and organization style, conflict handling strategies, problem identification, and solution methodologies. Past and existing performance-inhibiting factors for the most part were not caused by union intransigence or a lack of middle or lower level supervisory competence. These important factors seemed reasonably affirmative. The issue was, most basically, one of leadership at the top and its organization-wide impact. At the time of the study, the management team, or important segments of it, was somewhat demoralized, emasculated, and fearful. It was clear that only the immediate physical departure of the previous owner and total support for the new general manager's already aggressively determined actions to take charge would restore management confidence. There was a need to deliberately empower managers and supervisors at all levels, and to show them how to effectively use their power. Most were long accustomed to unquestioning obedience and to carrying out orders exactly. As examples of specific problems, there were substantive difficulties in the areas of management succession, potential promotability of existing staff, sales-marketing teamwork, a very high turnover of hourly workers, poor recruiting, selection, and employment processes, insufficient sales force motivation, supervision, and control, ineffective public relations efforts, and other issues.

The transcendent problem was to restore badly shattered managerial confidence and self-esteem. The new general manager was, we believed, capable of dealing with the specific difficulties noted. But so long as the previous owner remained, the new general manager's position would be extraordinarily awkward and powerless as would the roles of virtually all other managers and supervisors. It is important to recognize that these problems had a greater impact on the large primary operation than on the smaller remote plants.

One Remote Plant

This was a relatively small plant, although it had a very large vending service operation. With over 10,000 vendors in place, delivery and repair functions are vital. The manager was well-suited to his role and seemed to be doing an effective job. He appeared to have good control of the operation.

One key supervisor was described as quick to give credit to others and to praise them publicly for good work. He was regularly said to be very effective in delegating both responsibility and authority. He was seen as tough and demanding, but had the loyalty and respect of most employees. Both this supervisor and the manager received high marks from the hourly employees. Company-union relations were quite good, although we suspected that the shop steward would be a tough and effective negotiator. Both of these management people permitted and actively encouraged employees at all levels to "take charge, make decisions, and get it done." Neither was described as easygoing, but both were said to be supportive of those who sought out extra responsibilities and were accepting of occasional failures. Both of these supervisors deliberately empowered others.

Less positively, a second supervisor was described as technically excellent, but as showing sudden flashes of anger—almost rage—at mistakes. He often used a dictatorial manner, which turned a good many employees against him. He was clearly seen as less effective than the other supervisors. Especially in training new employees, he was described as less than adequate despite his strong technical ability and a willingness to take on and effectively perform almost any job himself. Indeed, the combination of autocratic style, anger at mistakes, and not trusting others to perform effectively all worked to greatly limit the expression of influence and power by others.

It seemed that there were significant economies of money and time to be realized by allowing this plant to perform more of its own truck maintenance and repair. We repeatedly saw situations where permitting this plant to perform more repairs would have avoided significant costs. The main plant's garage operation exercised unilateral control over what work could or could not be handled in other plants. Some control, especially of major repairs such as engine installations, seemed reasonable. But the present level of control was unrealistic. Mechanics in this particular plant wanted the opportunity to become proficient on a broader range of vehicles and problems. They wanted to personally and directly influence and affect published indicators like vehicle "down time" and repair cost. They wanted the power to achieve meaningful goals.

Main Plant

The main plant is an attractive well-maintained facility. It is so spread out that regular contact and communication among management group members and various plant functions is both difficult and very important.

Controller's Organization.
This organization seemed well-managed. Its members expressed both general satisfaction and, particularly, feelings of achievement. The controller's function had a relatively sophisticated analysis and reporting capability. The function was uniformly viewed as capable, powerful, and very helpful by other departments. The supervisors were seen as professional in approach and effective in providing data. There was considerable question, especially in sales, whether the data provided were used as effectively as they might be.

The previous owner rarely used the capabilities and recommendations of the controller's department and requested little sophisticated financial analysis. Nearly every employee in the department was delighted with the increased responsibility, impact, and influence of the department under the new ownership even though more difficult work was required. As one financial analyst said:

> What I do makes a difference now. I've had to relearn some techniques I haven't used in years. Its great to know that my recommendations are wanted and carry some weight.

Operations Department. The operations manager's retirement was only a few years away, and no suitable replacement had been identified. The maintenance and repair garage seemed in generally sound condition. There was, however, a need for consistent guidance concerning sales of older trucks, maintenance, and purchasing practices. In this department, as in many others, historically inconsistent, autocratic direction and inadequate leadership from the founder had been the norm. The operations manager tried to provide leadership, but his role was a difficult one—especially when the owner bypassed managers and supervisors to deliver important orders and instructions to lower level employees. It had not been at all unusual for the owner to contradict instructions given to employees by the operations and garage managers, usually without their knowledge. Managers and supervisors at all levels felt helpless and, in fact, had minimal influence over events important to the performance of their departments.

Employee turnover in production was extraordinary. Often people were employed only to leave within a few days. When additional people were needed, employees were sometimes asked to encourage friends "who would fit in" to apply. All too often, prospective hires were turned away at the front entrance on the grounds that there were no openings. Clearly, these problems incurred significant costs and created a less-than-desirable community image.

The near absence of communication between groups and departments often meant that neither department could adequately fulfill its mission. People in nearly every department said they felt helpless to change the situation. Many employees and managers had adopted behavior intended solely to preserve their jobs and security. They withdrew from active involvement as their ability to cause change and improvement was more and more frustrated.

Sales-Marketing. These two functions had not worked well together. Historically, they reported separately to the founder. It seemed essential that the two departments be more closely integrated and guided by a single manager. Relationships between the two departments were neither productive nor satisfying. Many employees described unresolved conflicts as common. Members of each organization seemed to put a lot of energy into winning some point of concession from the other—often the result was minimal commitment to establishing and meeting business objectives. It almost seemed that the founder had deliberately avoided defining roles and expectations for employees in the two departments. Employees and managers saw themselves as "unable" or "not permitted" to even try to resolve the issues.

> Sure, we've got bad problems between sales and marketing. Neither one of us gets much done. But you better not ever say so.

In sales, there was inadequate supervision of the route salesmen in many instances. There was noticeably less interest in achievement and accomplishment than in similar organizations of the parent company. Many managers simply did not know how to supervise and motivate others. Even more important, the pervasive management approach encouraged and rewarded self-protective behavior—not achievement.

There was some question about whether there were enough managers because many were forced to operate primarily as fill-in drivers, rather than true supervisors. This condition meant that the managers were often without contact, control, or power over the activities of their subordinates. Yet, senior level managers regularly drove throughout the franchise area inspecting the performance of the route salesmen. Managers were often berated by their bosses for the actions of salesmen they knew nothing about.

Contests and similar incentives had been discontinued in sales at the direction of the previous owner. They were missed, especially by those drivers who seemed to be highly achievement-oriented.

In some important departments, then, there were many key employees who felt unable to influence significant aspects of their working lives. Too many had adopted a withdrawn, security-oriented posture, and business performance lagged. As is often the case, new ownership brought sudden, sometimes dramatic change.

Some plant organizations and individuals reeled under new reporting requirements, while a few others were coping reasonably well. In the latter category, the accounting function appeared to be making orderly, effective progress. Its members seemed to understand the need for the various reports and felt they could get help rapidly from parent company corporate staff.

In the former category, the operations group seemed almost at a panic stage. They felt that many reporting demands from corporate were useless, trivial, and duplicated by reports already prepared by the plant controller's organization. The plant's operations supervisors said they were not supervising but acting mainly as clerks for the parent company's executives. Several attributed the turnover problem in operations to this decrease in day-to-day employee contact. They were convinced that they already had adequate data available internally to effectively control their operations function. Some believed that corporate operations "empire building" resulted in the plant operations group being required to produce analyses and reports of doubtful validity and utility.

When people feel essentially powerless, self-respect ebbs. A low level of self-esteem often shows up in organizations as finger-pointing, unquestioning obedience, unresolved conflicts, and a reduced ability to either initiate or respond to change effectively.

Summary

Several major characteristics of the management style and history of this operation warrant comment. First, there was greatly restricted access to performance data about the operation. Financial information was considered to be privileged information. It was available to even the most senior levels of management in incomplete form. While some information should obviously be restricted, nearly all supervisors and managers were starved for information. Because they received so little data, there was distrust of top management and a very active "grapevine."

When we are without dependable information or the skills to use it, we cannot be influential. We will have little ability to successfully guide, control, or anticipate events. When our need and desire for influence is frustrated, self-esteem suffers and we become increasingly concerned with shielding and protecting ourselves. As we have seen, that is exactly what happened.

Closely related to the restricted availability of data, decision-making was also very tightly controlled by upper management. Experience with decision-making was shallow in lower and middle level management. Most managers and supervisors felt essentially powerless, even within their own functions and departments.

A third set of characteristics was the communication patterns within the organization. Most communications, though very restricted, went only from upper management down. Very little information went from lower management to upper levels of the organization. Moreover, lateral communication between and among groups and departments was severely limited. Few employees even in managerial positions, knew what other departments did, even though these departments were highly interdependent. Teamwork was far below that needed for good organizational performance.

Note the power style, as reflected in limited access to information, tight control, and decisions made only at high organization levels. A top-down, one-way communication pattern was also evident. These are all characteristics of organizations operated like closed, rather than open, systems. Such actions make even key employees essentially powerless. Their self-respect falters as does organization performance.

GENERAL MANAGER'S FEEDBACK TO EMPLOYEES ABOUT THE ORGANIZATIONAL SURVEY

Shortly after this preliminary study, a detailed employee opinion survey was prepared and administered. Confidentiality of individual responses was guaranteed, and virtually all employees completed the questionnaire. The general manager shared some of his own perceptions and the key survey results in a letter to each employee. The near absence of personal power and influence below the very top levels is clearly described in his own words:

> During December, each employee of our operation was given the opportunity to complete a survey giving his opinions about the organization. I want to share with you the major problems we found and tell you about strategies to resolve these as well as other problems.
>
> 1. Numerous examples were found of an *inability or unwillingness to share and use information* concerning the effectiveness of the organization. This is obviously a management responsibility. Examples include unused computer reports, no shared responsibility for cost control, and lack of timely response to customer complaints.
>
> 2. Throughout the organization, *every* department indicated that employees are *not able to influence management* with their ideas and suggestions. Most managers very seldom ask for employees' ideas and suggestions. The survey shows that you have many ideas for better ways to do your jobs.

3. Somewhat to our surprise, we found that you see *problems which go unresolved* for long periods of time. The eventual effect of this seems to be a tolerance for low-level performance by allowing the problems to continually get in the way of completing work assignments.

4. Many of you are *confused about your specific responsibilities* and how those responsibilities overlap with other departments. We even found some examples of employees who do not know who their immediate boss is.

5. Decisions have historically been made only at the senior levels of management in our company. While this is not new information, we learned very clearly from the survey that middle and lower management, as well as employees, want more influence on decisions which affect their jobs.

> We have identified a list of problems which need to be resolved. Some of them are "quick fix" solutions and some will take longer to resolve. You will begin to see in the near future many of these "quick fix" problems taken care of, and you will be given information about the strategies to resolve the larger problems. I have instructed our senior managers to begin resolving these long-range problems during the next year. They have already been given significant, detailed information concerning their specific areas of responsibility. They will immediately begin meeting with their personnel to view the problems in detail, to establish priorities for resolving these problems, and to establish responsibility and target dates for their resolution. As this begins to occur, you should anticipate *hearing in more detail* what problems have been identified that affect your specific area. Some of you may be asked to *participate in either identifying solutions to these problems or in working on a task force* to resolve some of these problems.
>
> I am looking forward to the challenge of responding to the problems you have identified and to improving our operation in order to make this a better place to work. Thank you for your cooperation in completing the survey and for the honesty and frankness reflected in your written comments.

Dramatic change can be seen in the general manager's approach of involving employees in solution identification and task forces. Shortly after this, a plan was adopted to significantly improve the performance of the operation through deliberate enhancement of the self-esteem of its members. There were eight critical steps in the process, which were ex-

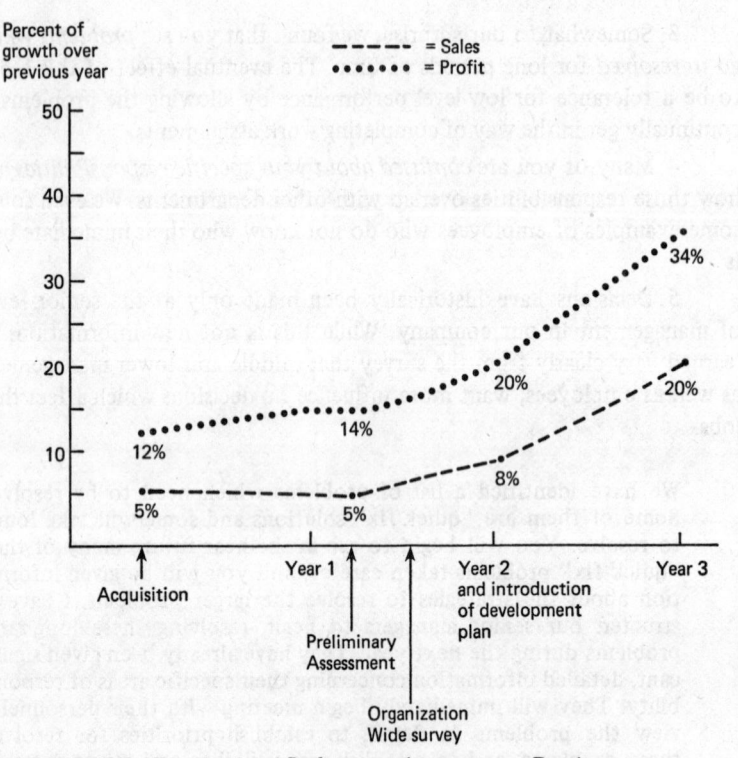

FIGURE 13.2. Organizational Performance Improvement Results.

pected to be completed in about a year. In fact, the process required about sixteen months, but the results were excellent, as shown in Figure 13.2.

The steps in the plan for organizational improvement follow and are given as they were originally proposed and subsequently implemented under the careful guidance of the new general manager.

Plan for Strategic Development

1. Results of the assessment/survey process will be shared and explored in detail with the general manager and his key staff. At the same meeting, the report of potentially actionable items will be reviewed. All items will be jointly prioritized. Those items warranting immediate action will be assigned to one or another of the staff for near-term resolution.

Possible actions, consequences, responsibilities, and expected completion dates should be set and published on the most pressing items. Internal communication of such actions is important and should be discussed and responsibility assigned.

Individuals or task forces should also be assigned to study and prepare recommendations for the more complex, long-range or low-priority items. These individuals or groups should be assigned dates to report findings and recommend actions to the general manager and his staff. Those responsible for each item should be encouraged to seek out whatever resources they require so that the type and extent of these resources can be discussed and determined.

It will be important to publish within the *entire* organization the nature of each significant project undertaken, those responsible, and expected completion dates. Employees who desire to contribute thoughts, data, or ideas should be encouraged to do so.

2. Each key manager will be trained and encouraged in feeding survey results back to all employees within his area of responsibility. He should actively seek and write down for further consideration the views, examples, ideas, and suggestions elicited from employees during this process. Once again, several sessions will be needed in each major functional area. The process, while critical, is not initially an easy one for many managers. Help, guidance, and assistance will be necessary until managers become comfortable with their expanded influence and power.

3. During the process of setting the organization's course in many areas, the roles, expectations, and responsibilities of many top level executives will require definition and renegotiation. This is a most significant and difficult step and will require some specific decisions about individuals, functions, required behaviors, benchmarks, and the like. The survey data explored in Step One, information from the employee feedback process and the top level objective-setting sessions when coupled with this "structuring process" will result in a consistent, planned, organizationally cohesive thrust.

4. Data from the survey, from the top executive group (Step One) and feedback from the employees in each functional area will immediately suggest some important goals and objectives for the entire operation. The top team will meet to begin the process of defining specifically these and other future objectives for the company. This joint goal-setting process

will be unfamiliar and, perhaps, uncomfortable for some so that support and help should be readily available.

5. The four steps outlined above set the stage by providing a top level thrust, structure and mission. But they do not provide adequately for the inclusion and commitment of lower level supervisors and others who are truly the key people in the operation.

A. From the objectives, goals, and agreements reached in earlier steps, each top staff executive will prepare himself to meet with all supervisors in his area of responsibility. Initially, he should meet with each subordinate manager to consider in detail:

(1) The survey-employee feedback findings and suggested solutions as they relate to the subordinate manager's responsibilities. Jointly, they will determine the actions required of the subordinate manager.
(2) Any changes in the executive's role and departmental structure or function that impact the subordinate manager and his area.
(3) The overall organization objectives and goals that are agreed on.
(4) The specific performance expectations the senior manager has for his subordinates and the subordinate's improvement and developmental requirements.

B. In a joint, problem-solving and objective-setting meeting, all supervisors in the particular functional area should examine the survey data and determine how best to respond to each significant problem. These sessions should be chaired by the senior functional executive. Other executives may be appropriate attendees as well. Once again, responsibilities for corrective action will be assigned and completion dates determined.

This process will result in determining some important functional and/or departmental objectives. Still other objectives will result as the functional supervisory team decides how best to contribute to overall organization objectives. In essence, this process will resemble that described earlier wherein the top executive group—a horizontal slice of the organization—is engaged in a joint objective-setting. The major conceptual difference is that the functional/departmental process involves vertical slices of the organization. The result of Step Five will be a supervisory group that is fully informed about all significant organization-wide goals, aware of and committed to departmental goals, and individually involved in causing improvement and change in the fundamental processes of the organization. Through these events, supervisors will gain much greater and more visible power and influence. They will come to share ownership of both the data and all relevant objectives.

6. On a department-by-department basis, managers and supervisors will meet with small groups of employees to explain company and departmental objectives and any changes in roles, procedures, and expectations determined during previous steps in the development process.

During these and subsequent small group meetings, employee suggestions and ideas from the survey-feedback will be shared. The departmental supervisor will explain what the management group has decided to do about each problem area, who is responsible, and the expected completion dates.

Throughout these several steps, there will be many opportunities for internal, employee-oriented communications. This internal communication effort is important and should regularly receive top level support and follow-through.

7. After two or more interfacing departments or functions have satisfactorily concluded Step Five, appropriate supervisors and managers from the two groups should meet to share their organizational objectives, priorities, roles, and problems. Essentially these are horizontal slices of the organization, spanning groups whose members must interact effectively if the objectives of each are to be realized. Conflicts, disagreements, and uncertainties will inevitably arise about the interacting roles, responsibilities, and objectives of the separate component groups. Redefinition and renegotiation will be required, but the result will be a much clearer understanding of the expectations, requirements, and responsibilities of each group. To a significant extent, these are cross-functional or cross-departmental team building sessions with improved bottom line performance as the result.

8. After nine months to a year, a second employee survey will provide guidance for any necessary mid-course corrections.

Your Analysis of the Eight-Step Plan

Refer back to your answers to the study questions on page 99, and consider the organization improvement plan just described. How do the various steps in the plan relate to the following considerations?

1. The self-esteem of employees, supervisors, and managers?
2. Esteem available from *each* of the four sources?
3. The overall amount of personal power and influence permitted and used?
4. Characteristics of open vs. closed systems?

Improvement Plan Summary

The improvement steps provided employees at all levels with many opportunities to project their power and influence. They were given power in the form of information. They were deliberately empowered as their views, ideas, and suggestions were vigorously solicited and acted upon. They gained influence as they sorted out and redefined their individual roles and organization objectives. And they gained self-esteem because many of them served on project and task teams where achievements could be readily seen. The regular renegotiation of roles, expectations, and behavior greatly expanded the number and quality of relationships. Increased self-esteem resulted from increased feelings of being valued and cared about.

The esteem of the organization's members was enhanced as they experienced being valued, as they began to see visible achievements, and as they felt increasing personal power and influence. But the key was the deliberate empowering of as many employees as possible. This factor caused the organization system to become much more open. The previously rigid, bureaucratic, and top-down use of power gave way to the use of varied power styles.

Within about six months, the organization came to act much more like an open rather than a closed system. As the plan unfolded, an amazing range of unusual and unconventional approaches were suggested, adopted, and implemented. The principle of equifinality was clearly operating in many functions and departments. A considerable number and variety of feedback loops were created, and previously ignored information was willingly shared and rapidly attended to. The feedback principle also was visible.

The lesson was clear. To most effectively help an organization become a more open system, its members must first be allowed opportunities to project and see the result of increased personal power and influence. The outcome will be improved individual feelings of worth, value, and self-esteem. As shown in Figure 13.2, another result is usually a significantly improved level of organizational performance.

chapter fourteen

Power and stress

Some of the behaviors and feelings that go along with low self-esteem have already been described:

1. Rigid behavior patterns
2. Withdrawal and lack of involvement
3. Fear and anxiety
4. Reduced commitment
5. Sadness and depression
6. Little risk-taking; much self-protection
7. Harried and frantic behaviors
8. Little real listening
9. Reliance on the past; low creativity
10. Short tempered and prickly

When someone shows these behaviors and describes feelings like those listed above, we often attribute it to stress. This is natural because stress, when it goes unattended, can reduce self-esteem; and low self-esteem makes us still more susceptible to the effects of stress producing situations around us. Figure 14.1 shows a likely relationship and sequence between stress and self-esteem. Of course, under some conditions the sequence can be greatly compressed. We can examine stress at behavioral and feeling levels without becoming too involved in the physiological processes.

We have all probably experienced this process: work piles up, the boss is clearly displeased, the car broke down on the way to work, and . . . Our worlds are full of stressors (1). Even before we are consciously aware of it, the effects of all the various stressors pile up and are at some level perceived, although often not at a conscious level (2).

Our bodies respond by stimulating some internal processes and inhibiting others (3). Adrenalin is released and our hearts seem to pound. If it goes far enough, blood pressure rises, pulse accelerates, pupils dilate, and we are ready to run or fight. At that point (4) we begin to know clearly that something is wrong. We may feel anxious and fearful, jittery and nervous. We begin to make mistakes, become short-tempered with little reason, and eat and sleep less well than usual. Some of us will withdraw and become less communicative while others may respond with almost frenzied activity. But for nearly all who experience significant, unrelieved stress, strong feelings of powerlessness (5) develop. We feel helpless and unable to cope with the avalanche of events, stimuli, and

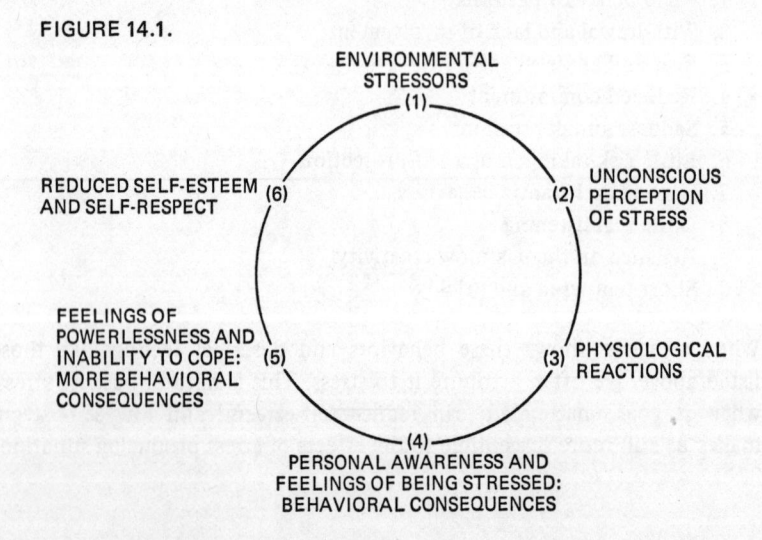

FIGURE 14.1.

(1) ENVIRONMENTAL STRESSORS
(2) UNCONSCIOUS PERCEPTION OF STRESS
(3) PHYSIOLOGICAL REACTIONS
(4) PERSONAL AWARENESS AND FEELINGS OF BEING STRESSED: BEHAVIORAL CONSEQUENCES
(5) FEELINGS OF POWERLESSNESS AND INABILITY TO COPE: MORE BEHAVIORAL CONSEQUENCES
(6) REDUCED SELF-ESTEEM AND SELF-RESPECT

demands. It is too much, too fast to handle. Our emotions and thought processes are in a turmoil, and we are not at all sure what we can or should do.

As we feel more powerless and less able to influence the situation, we begin to doubt ourselves. We become an increasingly harsh critic of our own feelings and actions. Our self-respect declines (6) and we may become sad, depressed, angry, anxious, or all of these. With a reduction in our self-esteem, we are even less likely to take the actions necessary to achieve self-positive feelings from the four sources. We may not only *feel* powerless, we may *act* powerless as well.

At that point, we are easy prey to other potentially stressful situations and events (1). Little annoyances seem to be major hurdles. A thoughtless or even innocent word or act by another seems to be a condemnation. And the cycle can continue to build. As we have already seen, when we are unusually stressed we will tend to rely on and overuse our main, or primary, power style. Under such conditions, it is hard to stop and reflect or to deliberately select another way of influencing the people and events around us. That same locked-down rigidity can prevent us from acting in ways that could relieve the stress. It can prevent our seeking self-esteem from one or more of the four sources at exactly the time we most need to feel valuable, in control, and worthwhile.

Feelings of being unusually stressed, overwhelmed, inflexible, or powerless are signals that it is time to take deliberate action to restore our sense of self-respect.

Any major change or a series of seemingly minor changes can cause stress. This is true even when the changes appear positive to others. For example, family gatherings, holidays, and job promotions all seem to be positive events. But all of these can, and often do, cause stress responses. For many of us, our systems adapt to frequent stressful conditions by staying aroused so that we may often, or even usually, be at a rather high stress level. In our complex society, with its restrictions and norms against expressing emotions, our systems can stay geared up to run or fight over long periods. Prescriptively, we can say that when you and I feel unusually stressed we should look first to the use of our personal power.

1. What power style am I using?
2. Is the way I am using my influence stuck on just one style?
3. Am I overusing a particular style?
4. Would one of the other approaches be more successful?

Next, we can quietly examine our feelings of self-esteem, our sense of personal worth and value, and our self-respect.

1. From which of the four sources of self-esteem do I usually gain the most positive and affirmative feelings about myself?
2. What is that potential esteem source doing for me right now?
3. How much am I gaining from the other esteem sources?

Now we are in a position to deliberately decide how and in what ways we will use our influence to gain self-positive feelings from each source.

1. What potential source(s) of self-esteem will I concentrate on?
2. What, specifically, do I want to occur?
3. Which power style is most likely to achieve this objective?
4. What, specifically, must I do? How must I act? With whom must I interact?

Sometimes, these kinds of reflections may lead to the conclusion that the present environment or situation prevents us from gaining adequate self-esteem, no matter which power style is used. Such an examination may sometimes clearly show that only major change in some aspect of our lives will allow us to gain critically needed self-respect.

In such cases we might change our reflections and questions and begin to specify the characteristics of a desired *new* situation or environment where we can use our influence to gain more positive feelings about ourselves. The very act of deciding to change—specifically describing what to change and how—is a use of our personal influence and will begin to *increase* our feelings of worth and value.

In the work environment, there are not only the possible stressors of work load, noise, and a crowded environment. There are especially strong norms against expressing emotions. There is usually little opportunity to "burn off" stress and the bodily chemicals, like adrenalin, associated with it. Some progressive companies provide exercise rooms, jogging paths, and the like partly to aid employees in managing their stress.

Almost any work environment also imposes a good many controls that can add to stress. They can limit our personal influence, restrict opportunities to achieve, and sometimes produce an uncaring atmosphere. There are, for example, many policies and rules about who can do what that severely restrict one's freedom, power, and influence. There are almost certainly many unspoken rules or norms about how one is supposed to act, speak, and dress. These norms also restrict our freedom and our influence. Our roles as secretary, manager, keypunch operator, supervisor, chemist, or whatever can also be restricted because others have firm expectations about how we should, will, or ought to behave.

Paradoxically, roles that are fuzzy and ambiguous can also produce considerable pressure. In the absence of a reasonably clear definition of our role, and with only a vague idea of what others expect, we may feel very insecure and fearful of making a mistake. Achievement and accomplishment are hard, if not impossible, to see if we have no goals and only an indistinct idea of what is expected. It is easy in such situations to feel that no one values or cares about us. In our society there are many pressures for upward movement; to do better, get the better job and make more money. These pressures can add to stress. Executives and managers can experience all of these pressures—and a few others that go with the extra stripes of rank and position.

A good many people in senior-level positions find it very stressful to live up to the company image of what a manager should be. Heavy involvement in civic or political associations is often expected with the resulting loss of time to spend alone, with family, or with friends. Home ties are frequently severed or greatly weakened during the climb up the ladder. Company norms and expectations about where and how one should live not only limit one's freedom but can also impose economic pressures on even well-paid executives. Many executives have told me of feeling terribly lonely and isolated. They say they see the same people both socially and at work, and these are often people with whom they are in direct competition for the next highest level position. They often have few real friends. They describe how the company expects them to act, and with whom, and where. These upwardly mobile, ambitious people have often given up their personal power in return for material rewards.

With higher position, many feel great loneliness and fear of failure. Some describe their rise in terms of the cost to their personal values and ethics. Little involvement with spouse and children, questionable behavior to win praise and recognition, and disguised, hidden attacks on potential rivals for a better job are common examples of this cost. The cost is also figured in terms of self-respect and self-esteem. It is felt as unremitting pressure and stress.

Whether or not we are managers, many of us feel the pressure of middle-aged doubt when we confront the fact of our own mortality

FIGURE 14.2.

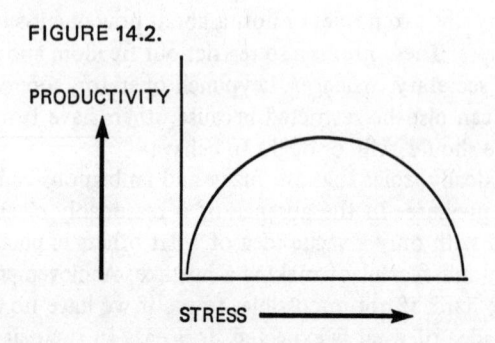

[Graph showing an inverted-U curve with PRODUCTIVITY on the vertical axis and STRESS on the horizontal axis.]

and ultimate powerlessness, and wonder whether our dreams and hopes will ever be realized. For many, fear of retirement and "letting go" are major sources of stress. Some organizations provide their employees with substantial preretirement advice. Some others make confidential personal and psychological counselling available to all employees on request.

The key to controlling stress lies in the use of our influence and power to gain essential self-esteem and self-respect. The issue is one of *controlling*, not eliminating stress, which is probably impossible. Moreover some stress, some pressure, is necessary for most of us to perform well. Too little stress, and minimal energy is invested; too much, and we need all our energy just to survive. At either extreme, little productive work will be done as shown in Figure 14.2.

Stress-caused behavior often seems to have a ripple or domino effect in the close interdependency of many organizations. One or two troubled people show some of the symptoms of stress. Before long, others are impacted. *They* begin to show some of the same signs, and the organization's productivity is in jeopardy. Some of these symptomatic behaviors are so obvious that they are often ignored, but others are more subtle. The sensitive manager or supervisor will be alert to these signs of possible individual stress on the job.

1. Looks upset
2. Frequent visits to the bathroom
3. Looks and acts sleepy
4. Change in posture; rigidity, slumping
5. Significant gain or loss of weight
6. Frequent visits to the medical department

7. Nervousness, agitation, pacing, jittery
8. Depression, sadness, apathy, crying
9. High sensitivity to even modest criticism
10. Increased irritability
11. Fatigue
12. Absenteeism, tardiness
13. Increased errors and mistakes
14. Changes in typical behavior; talkative person becomes quiet or a meticulous person becomes careless. Typical patterns may be exaggerated.
15. Increased consumption of pain relievers such as aspirin.

Think about some organization you know well. Do you see any of these behaviors? Do any of the people who work with you seem to be showing signs of stress? Are you?

As we have seen, stress is intimately related to feelings of powerlessness, and it ultimately decreases our self-esteem. Our complex lives put us into contact with many stress-producing events and conditions. The organizations where we spend so large a part of our lives present many pressures and potential sources of stress. Some stress seems necessary and is probably inevitable, but how can we use our power, our influence, to control stress?

Each of us already has many mechanisms for coping with stress. Those listed below have proven helpful to many people in both coping with and preventing some harmful effects of stress and pressure.

Build Self-Esteem

Deliberately increase your self-esteem through the exercise of your own influence. Set up and/or find opportunities to visibly accomplish and achieve; seek caring through affiliation with others; renew and act out your moral and ethical code.

It is not at all necessary that our achievements be large, awe-inspiring, or even known to others. Hobbies, yard work, and car repair are all used in this way by many people. An hour or two working on a model ship may serve the purpose. What works for you?

It isn't necessary to become a compulsive joiner to feel valued and cared about through affiliation with others. Our families and friends are available and can be enormously supportive if we choose to let them.

Work, church, and other associations can provide many opportunities to develop new and personally important relationships.

Politics and even running for office, advisory boards, commissions, charity work, families, and a host of other outlets exist for us to act upon our deeply held values and beliefs. These are situations where our philosophy is important. They are also situations where there are likely to be others who share our values.

Deliberately building one's self-esteem is particularly helpful because a reasonably high level of self-respect allows us to be less disturbed by potential pressure and stress. We are better able to deal effectively with stressful situations and events when we are secure in the knowledge of our personal worth and value.

Rest and Sleep

This may seem obvious, but the fact is that under high stress many people make little effort to get the rest they need. Moreover, many of us have trouble saying, "No" to reasonable requests for help or assistance from those we care about. Many managers don't consider turning down their organization's request to become involved in an endless array of civic projects. Others of us are downright compulsive about meeting all our obligations on or ahead of time. All of these are tiring and take time that can be deliberately used to prevent and deal more effectively with stress.

Planning and Rehearsal

We can exercise our ability to influence people and events by deciding what we want and planning exactly how we will go about meeting our desires. We can project our power by implementing the plan. Planning includes deciding on specific goals, evaluating the consequences of total success and total failure, describing the actions we must take and anticipating both potential barriers and the resources we will need. It should also include feedback mechanisms so our progress can be tracked and midcourse corrections made.

Mental rehearsal can be a powerful way of reducing the potential stress of expected events. For example, many salesmen say they regularly rehearse how they will approach a particular prospect. They think about how they will present their product. They anticipate how they will deal with almost any conceivable objection, and they consider any extra inducements they can offer. All of this is rehearsal. The same process can be used in preparing for any possible difficult or stressful situation. Often, when we look at the worst possible consequences of doing something, much of our fear disappears because the worst isn't nearly so bad after all.

Suppose you know that your boss is very angry about something you have done. He sends word that he wants to see you in his office at 9 A.M. tomorrow. You can simply allow yourself to grow more and more fearful, stressed, and powerless. Or you might mentally rehearse the situation as it seems likely to happen. First, you could think about the worst possible outcome. Perhaps you'll be fired! Upon reflection, you may decide that being out of a job would be difficult, but probably not disastrous. The calming effect of that realization is likely to permit you to effectively use your determination—your influence—to mentally rehearse how you will cool your boss down and improve his view of your actions.

Rehearsal and anticipation are ways of deliberately using power to influence events and to reduce stress. The process reduces the chance we'll be caught unawares, and it allows us to play out our fears, concerns, and emotions in private before the fact. In this way we can become both calmer and more effective in the actual situation.

Physical Activity

The same sophistication and complexity all around us that can produce great pressure and stress also keep us from dealing with stress by expressing our strong feelings and emotions openly. Our early ancestors probably picked up a rock and let fly at the cause of their fear and anger. But strong emotional expression is simply not expected or permitted in most organizations. The boss's displeasure may have the same effect for us as sight of the saber-toothed tiger just beyond the fire did for that long ago ancestor. We want to run or fight but can do neither.

Physical activity not only keeps us healthy and better able to cope; it helps us sleep and eat better. Moreover, physical activity helps metabolize body chemicals that go along with stress. Physical activity need not be especially strenuous. Running, while very popular, is not for everyone. Brisk walking and swimming, for example, seem to be just as helpful. Before engaging in any strenuous exercise program, it is wise to check with your doctor.

Attention to Diet

When we feel a lot of pressure we can't deal with effectively, many of us will pay much less attention to what, when, and how much we eat and drink. Crash or fad diets may temporarily make you feel better, but many ultimately fail. That failure can add to stress. Too much, too little, or the wrong kind will add to problems. There are special stress diets and vitamin supplements. Most of us probably don't need these if we are reasonably prudent and careful. Once again, if you are unsure of what a proper diet should be for someone with your particular needs, age, and physique, check with your doctor or other professional.

Biofeedback

In this process, one or more indicators of our physiological and emotional state are painlessly measured, amplified, and presented in some easy-to-understand form. Many of us can then learn ways of changing that indicator reading. For example, with the right equipment we can easily measure the Galvanic Skin Response—an indicator of the activity of the autonomic nervous system. When we learn to change the GSR meter reading, it indicates that conditions, such as skin resistance, have changed. In this way, many people have learned to deliberately control blood pressure and other indicators with little or no reliance on drugs.

Many physicians and psychologists regularly use biofeedback with their patients. Personal use equipment is now small, easy-to-use, and costs in the range of a good quality portable music system ($100–$200).

Meditation or Relaxation

This is not the place for a detailed examination of the many meditation techniques available. These have been described in readily available books and articles. The process amounts to a deliberate unfocussing of one's mind and thoughts, a detachment from problems, worries, events, and people. The result, for many, is deep relaxation and refreshment. A good many executives, for instance, are finding that twenty to thirty minutes twice a day greatly improves their feeling of well-being, concentration, and productivity.

Therapy

There are various short-duration psychotherapies available today that have helped many people cope more effectively with pressure and stress. Many people think of psychotherapy as only for the seriously ill or as a long process, but neither condition is necessarily true any longer.

Psychologists and psychiatrists, among others, provide these services. Progressive companies are increasingly understanding and regularly encourage employees to use such services when they are appropriate. Many benefit plans cover all or most of the cost. Apart from any human concerns, it's just sound business.

Programs

There are a variety of stress-control programs offered by many firms. Most of these programs seem to be two or three days long. Some are excellent, but investigate before you buy.

I'm sure you can add to this list of ways to cope with pressure and stress. These seem to be generally effective for most people.

Notice that each method allows and requires you to use your power and influence to do or change something. Your decision to act and the process of deliberately implementing your plan is an expression of your power. That expression, by itself, will begin to build your self-esteem and will help you handle stress more effectively.

chapter fifteen

Constraints and approaches to improving employee self-esteem

A major problem for many organizations is how to create self-esteem producing conditions within the existing structure. A number of discrete techniques have been outlined in the case study in Chapter 13. To improve job satisfaction and organizational performance, management training, organization development, human relations approaches, quality circles, participative management, job enrichment, and teambuilding have all been effective. All of these techniques are useful, but without other changes they often do not succeed as well as they might.

The issue is not satisfaction with the *job* but, rather, satisfaction with one's self, that is, self-esteem. As we have seen, when employee self-esteem is high, so is individual and organizational performance. It seems clear that of the four sources of self-esteem, the largest deficit for most of us is the relatively low level of power and influence we think we can exert.

To improve self esteem, then, we must empower people at all levels to a significantly greater degree than has been the case in most organizations. As they are often used, the specific techniques just noted do not, by themselves, directly and explicitly empower employees. When such techniques work well, it is because the particular technique, whatever its specific attributes, is fully accepted and supported as a mechanism for empowering employees by high-level managers. For example, management training can be most effective only in the presence of an expressed and supported philosophy of relative individual and unit autonomy and freedom of action. When such a philosophy is not present, or is only marginally supported, the newly gained perceptions and skills will not be used. Collaborative approaches, unless fully supported and accepted as a way of increasing *individual* achievement, power, and rewards, will not generally succeed either.

When people in significant leadership positions use and support these techniques with full recognition and an expressed desire to give organization members more personal influence and power, those techniques generally work well. The success of the particular technique relies not so much on its content but on the personal commitment and philosophy of one or more people in authority positions. This support can be tenuous and short-lived in many organizations.

What is needed is an approach that deliberately empowers people and thereby builds self-esteem. Moreover, we need an approach that is less dependent (none can be fully independent) on the philosophy and commitment of one top-level person.

Thus, a long-term, successful approach must be relatively embedded in the organization. It must be less dependent on the philosophical approval of one or two top-level leaders and more a part of the enduring aspects of the organization's existence. And, as already discussed, it must empower people so that they can gain an improved sense of personal worth and value, of self-esteem. We must actively intervene in the structure of the official, larger organization to formally create an alternative, parallel problem-solving and reporting structure.

As has long been recognized, most organizations have an informal, or shadow structure. This informal organization has a more or less definable structure, and it has leadership. It often has a host of mechanisms for spreading information (the grapevine), setting behavioral and output quotas (informal norms), and disciplining members who don't conform (ostracism). An informal organization exists in nearly every office and plant, though it varies markedly in cohesion and visibility from one organization to another. Ultimately, the informal organization serves the self-esteem of those involved. Usually the emergent or informal organization seems to exist primarily to show members that they are cared about and valued by others. The informal communications system, casual groupings for lunch or at work breaks, and picking up the load for a fellow employee are all evidences that one is cared about.

The informal organization is, then, an example of people seeking to gain self-esteem from one of the four sources: being cared about and valued. In an organization characterized by managerial or supervisory remoteness from employees, the informal organization may serve to significantly bolster employee self-esteem. The informal organization is one kind of change introduced by employees into, or on top of, the formal company structure. It helps overcome impersonality, one of the negative aspects of a bureaucratic structure noted on page 75.

The modern large organization often acts to greatly reduce a person's feeling that he or she can have influence over surrounding conditions and situations. The pyramid structure itself reduces self-esteem by promoting feelings of powerlessness. The result is often less-than-adequate individual and organization productivity.

Nor are matrix management structures often of much help in enhancing self-esteem. A matrix system is typically organized around two dimensions. Along one dimension are separate projects or tasks and their leadership. Along another are particular skill or competency departments, or groups and their managements. A particular employee may, for example, receive direction from one or more managers along each dimension. It is easy to see why many people in a matrix system feel so helpless, why their self-esteem is low, and why such organizations often perform poorly.

The dominant, pyramid-shaped, bureaucratic organizational structure is not going to disappear. It has, in fact, proven very efficient in the production of goods and services. Even though its weaknesses are becoming increasingly evident, why should it disappear? Finally, there is simply too much investment in personal and economic terms to expect the managerial pyramid to significantly change in most organizations.

We might however, consider inserting an alternative structure that can successfully coexist with the formal structure and become equally and visibly a part of the organization's life and reporting relationships. The alternative structure can not be one that is defined as in *opposition* to the formal, pyramidal structure. If the alternative structures proposed are seen to be opposed to existing institutions, an adversary relationship will quickly develop. The result may be no more than another employee vs. management confrontation. The alternative structure suggested here is not the same as the informal structure already discussed. It is a defined structure with specific organization objectives. Its primary purpose is to empower its members.

A successful alternative structure must include some of those who occupy significant positions in the traditional hierarchy. In this way, the existing pyramidal system is represented and can support change and improvement as suggested by the alternative system. That power gives legitimacy to the alternative, parallel organization.

Much has been written about the use of "quality circles" in Japanese industry. These are small groups of employees who regularly meet to consider changes and improvements. The effectiveness and, indeed, the very existence of this method depends on the fact that the circles are recognized, visible, and legitimized structures embedded in the life of the organization. They also have regular access to those in top positions. The method is effective ultimately because it deliberately empowers the participants. Interestingly, quality circles seem to have been an American invention, accepted and developed especially by the Japanese and recently embraced by important segments of U.S. business and industry.

Suggestion committees and task forces are other approaches often used as parallel organizations. For example, consider a typical hierarchy in business, industry or the public sector. The different *levels* in the particular organization, such as production employee, engineer, accountant, manager, supervisor, and so forth, are indicated in Figure 15.1.

The letters indicate different *functions* or departments such as production, accounting, or engineering. It doesn't matter what the specific levels are called or what the functions are; most organizations have a structure not too different from that outlined.

For example, C 1-3 might be financial experts, while E 1-3 could be engineers. Organizationally, both groups are at about the same level in the hierarchy even though their skills and functions are different. Positions labelled B 1-4 might be approximately equal senior managers who supervise and direct a large group of subordinate supervisors and employees dedicated to a major function like engineering, production, or finance.

Ideally, a parallel organization should meet the following criteria:

1. It should have units small enough to become interpersonally close, cohesive, and communicative.

FIGURE 15.1. A Typical Organization Structure.

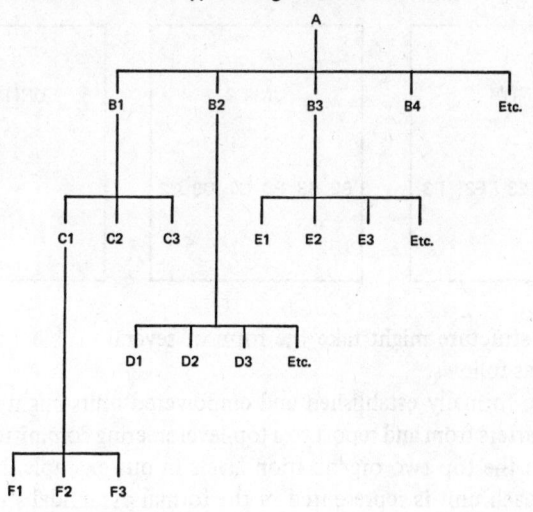

2. Membership from all major constituencies and necessary bases of knowledge should be represented, so that people feel included and resources are available for achievement.

3. Membership should include at least one person with significant clout and "position power" in the traditional structure. This helps empower members who know they have high-level access and support.

4. It should have reasonably clear goals so that changes and improvements can be made fairly rapidly and achievements can be seen.

5. Opportunities should exist for many employees at all levels to become involved in the unit.

Notice that these criteria, if met, provide for self-esteem from at least three of the four sources:

1. Visible power and influence over situations and events.
2. Achievement and accomplishment of personally important goals.
3. Evidence of being valued, recognized, and cared about.

FIGURE 15.2.

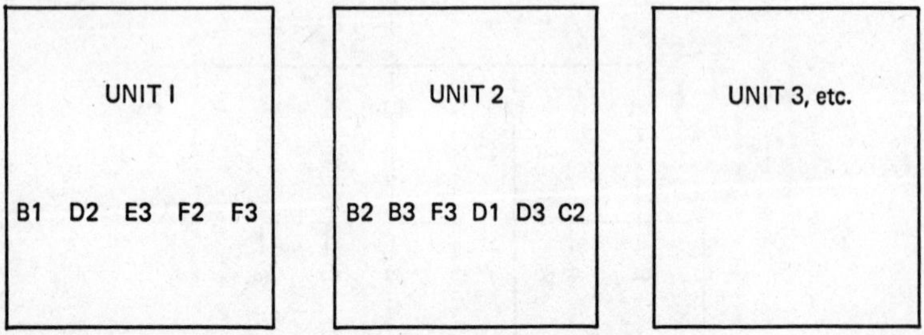

UNIT 1	UNIT 2	UNIT 3, etc.
B1 D2 E3 F2 F3	B2 B3 F3 D1 D3 C2	

A parallel structure might take the form of several problem solving units composed as follows:

These formally established and empowered units might receive their original charters from and report to a top-level steering committee composed of those in the top two organization levels in our example. Notice, however, that each unit is represented in the formal pyramidal structure by at least one senior level executive.

There are many alternatives to the structure outlined here. The exact form is not as important as meeting the criteria suggested with particular attention to deliberately empowering a substantial number of employees at all levels.

chapter sixteen

What is power?

So, what is power? It is our personal way of getting others to do what we want or causing things to happen as we wish so as to increase our own sense of self-esteem. The expression of personal power is itself a major source of self-esteem. But more than that, the use and projection of our personal power is the vehicle by which we gain self-esteem from the other three sources as well. Figure 16.1 below, is a graphic representation of the ideas we have already considered.

At Step (1) on the drawing we see that managers and others involved in guiding the actions of organizations have a fundamental choice: whether to treat organizations as closed or as open systems. If the choice is to deliberately and consistently permit and encourage organizations and their members to act as open systems, then four strategies (a)-(d) become appropriate. These strategies are appropriate precisely because they *are* characteristic of open systems.

As item (2) on the drawing shows, when such strategies are encouraged, individuals will be increasingly permitted to use their personal power in one or more of the six ways. The encouraged feedback processes from Step (1) will tend to reduce ineffective overuse of any one power style.

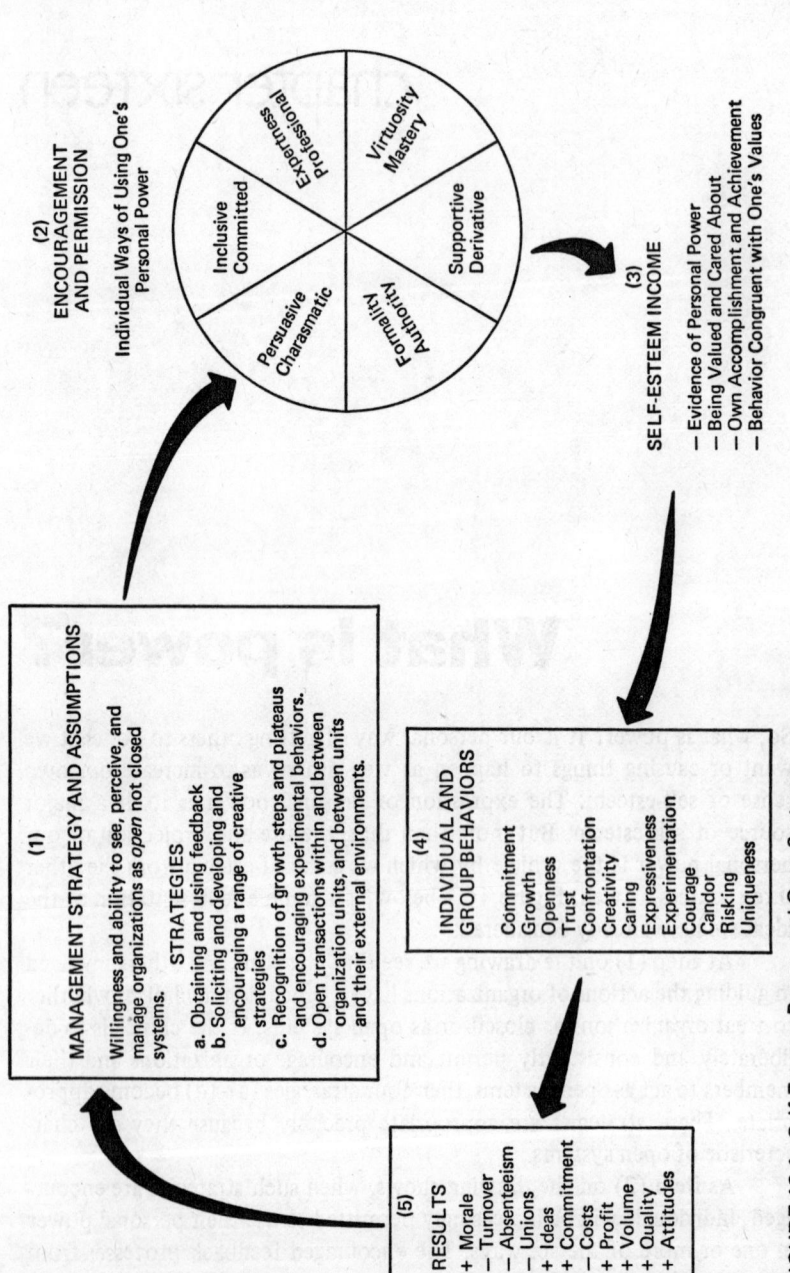

FIGURE 16.1. Self-Esteem, Power, and Open Systems.

(1) MANAGEMENT STRATEGY AND ASSUMPTIONS

Willingness and ability to see, perceive, and manage organizations as *open* not closed systems.

STRATEGIES
a. Obtaining and using feedback
b. Soliciting and developing and encouraging a range of creative strategies
c. Recognition of growth steps and plateaus and encouraging experimental behaviors.
d. Open transactions within and between organization units, and between units and their external environments.

(2) ENCOURAGEMENT AND PERMISSION

Individual Ways of Using One's Personal Power

- Virtuosity Mastery
- Supportive Derivative
- Formal Authority
- Persuasive Charasmatic
- Inclusive Committed
- Expertness Professionalness

(3) SELF-ESTEEM INCOME

— Evidence of Personal Power
— Being Valued and Cared About
— Own Accomplishment and Achievement
— Behavior Congruent with One's Values

(4) INDIVIDUAL AND GROUP BEHAVIORS

Commitment
Growth
Openness
Trust
Confrontation
Creativity
Caring
Expressiveness
Experimentation
Courage
Candor
Risking
Uniqueness

(5) RESULTS

+ Morale
− Turnover
− Absenteeism
− Unions
+ Ideas
+ Commitment
− Costs
+ Profit
+ Volume
+ Quality
+ Attitudes

As people begin to use power in their individualistic ways, they will use it to seek out self-esteem from one or more of the four sources, Step (3) in the diagram. The direction and thrust of the effort to gain self-esteem will be guided by the individual's values and beliefs.

At Step (4) we see some of the kinds of behaviors and attitudes that characterize individuals and organizations when self-esteem is high. These visible behaviors and the members' feelings of self-worth and value become the organization's climate, or culture. These kinds of results seem to precede "bottom line" changes which may not be evident for a year to eighteen months.

As such behaviors become widely shared throughout the plant, office, company, or department, some measurable results begin to be evident, as shown in Step (5). Morale increases (+), employee turnover decreases (-), costs decline (-), and so on, depending on the particular organization.

When individuals and whole organizations see clear evidence of the use of their power to achieve meaningful results, self-esteem increases and the organization behaves still more as an open system. The process resembles a spiral. At a personal level, when we use our own power successfully, we feel better about who we are. We become more receptive to feedback. We become more creative, communicative, and experimental. We risk growth and change. In other words, we can act more and more as open systems with the capacity for still more growth and renewal.

The direction for managers and others concerned about organization performance seems clear:

1. Manage individuals and organizations as the open systems they inherently are.

2. Permit and actively encourage the use and expression of each individual's personal power in the service of his or her own self-esteem.

3. Deliberately empower the largest number of employees possible, especially where previous management practices or structures may have greatly constrained use of their power.

4. Consider how you now use, or overuse, your power. Decide what changes seem appropriate.

As individuals, we also have choices. We can deliberately set about using our power and expanding the number of ways we use it to gain greater

136 / What is Power?

feelings of self-worth and value. With greater self-esteem, our behavior will include more of those characteristics listed under Step (4) in Figure 16.1, and we will become more personally effective in important parts of our lives. This process at a personal or organization level may seem a bit frightening. Growth and change are scary, but they are also exciting, challenging, and alive. The alternative is, for most of us, much worse.

You have the power. The choice of whether and how to use it is, as always, yours.

Bibliography

Ables, Billie S., and Brandsman, Jeffrey M. *Theory for Couples*. San Francisco: Jossey-Bass, Inc., Publishers, 1977.

Allport, Gordon. *Becoming: Basic Considerations for Psychology of Personality*. New Haven, Conn.: Yale University Press, 1955.

Argyris, Chris. *Interpersonal Competence and Organization Effectiveness*. Homewood, Ill.: Richard D. Irwin, Inc., 1962.

Atkinson, John W., ed., *Motives in Fantasy, Action and Society: A Method of Assessment and Study*. New York: D. Van Nostrand Company, 1958.

Bell, Gerald, D. *The Achievers: Six Styles of Personality and Leadership*. Chapel Hill, NC: Preston-Hill, Inc., 1973.

Berelson, Bernard, and Gary A. Steiner. *Human Behavior: An Inventory of Scientific Findings*. New York: Harcourt Brace Jovanovich, Inc., 1964.

Berle, Adolf A. *Power*. New York: Harcourt Brace Jovanovich, Inc., 1969.

Berne, Eric. *Transactional Analysis in Psychotherapy: A Systematic Individual and Social Psychiatry*. New York: Grove Press, Inc., 1961.

Bindra, Dalbir. *Motivation: A Systematic Reinterpretation*. New York: The Ronald Press Co., 1959.

138 / Bibliography

Bradshaw, Pete. *The Management of Self-Esteem.* Englewood Cliffs, N.J.: Prentice-Hall, Inc. 1981.

Cofer, C. N., and Appley, M. H. *Motivation: Theory and Research.* New York: John Wiley & Sons, Inc., 1964.

Cribbin, James J. *Effective Managerial Leadership.* New York: American Management Association, Inc., 1972.

Dittes, James E. "Attractiveness of Group as Function of Self-Esteem and Acceptance by Group." *Journal of Abnormal and Social Psychology,* Vol. LIX (1959) 77–82.

Drucker, Peter F. *Effective Executive.* New York: Harper & Row, Publishers, Inc., 1967.

Fagan, Joan, and Shepherd, Irmal Lee, eds. *Gestalt Therapy Now: Theory, Techniques, Applications.* New York: Harper & Row, Publishers, Inc., 1971.

Fendrock, John J. *Managing in Times of Radical Change.* New York: American Management Association, Inc., 1971.

Glasser, William. *Reality Therapy: A New Approach to Psychiatry.* New York: Harper & Row, Publishers, Inc., 1975.

Goffman, Erving. *The Presentation of Self In Everyday Life.* Woodstock, N.Y.: The Overlook Press, 1973.

Haldeman, H. R.; *The Ends of Power.* New York: Dell Publishing Co., Inc., 1978.

Hersey, Paul, and Blanchard, Kenneth. *Management of Organizational Behavior: Utilizing Human Resources.* Englewood Cliffs, N.J.: Prentice-Hall Publishing Co., Inc., 1969.

Herzberg, Frederick. *Work and the Nature of Man.* New York: World Publishing Co., 1966.

Herzberg, F. B., and Snyderman, Barbara. *The Motivation to Work,* 2nd ed. New York: John Wiley & Sons, Inc., 1959.

Hughes, Charles L. *Making Unions Unnecessary.* New York: Executive Enterprises Publications Co., Inc., 1976.

Janov, Arthur. *The Primal Scream: The Cure for Neurosis.* New York: Dell Publishing Co., Inc., 1970.

Katzell, R., and Yankelovich, D. *Work, Productivity and Job Satisfaction.* New York: New York University Press, 1975.

Kohn, Robert L., et al. *Organization Stress.* New York: John Wiley & Sons, Inc., 1964.

Korda, Michael. *Power—How to Get It, How to Use It.* New York: Ballantine Books, Inc., 1975.
LeShan, Eda J. *The Wonderful Crisis of Middle Age: Some Personal Reflections.* New York: Warner Books, 1973.
Levinson, Harry. *Psychological Man.* Cambridge, Mass.: The Levinson Institute, Inc., 1976.
Levinson, Harry, et al. *Men, Management and Mental Health.* Cambridge, Mass.: Harvard University Press, 1962.
Lockland, George T. *Grow or Die: The Unifying Principles of Transformation.* New York: Random House, Inc., 1973.
Lorenz, Konrad. *On Aggression.* New York: Bantam Books, Inc., 1967.
Machiavelli, N. *The Prince;* New York and Scarborough, Ontario: The New American Library, 1952.
Maslow, Abraham H. *Motivation and Personality.* New York: Harper & Row, Publishers, Inc., 1954.
———. *New Knowledge in Human Values.* New York: Harper & Row, Publishers, Inc., 1959.
———. *Toward a Psychology of Being.* Princeton, N.J.: D. Van Nostrand Company, 1962.
McCall, Morgan W. and Lombardo, Michael M. eds. *Leadership, Where Else Can We Go?* Durham, N.C.: Duke University Press, 1978.
McClelland, David C. *The Achievement Motive.* New York: Appleton-Century-Crofts, Publishers, 1953.
———. *Studies in Motivation.* New York: Appleton-Century-Crofts, Publishers, 1955.
———. *The Achieving Society.* New York: D. Van Nostrand Company, 1961.
Meister, David. *Behavioral Foundations of System Development.* New York: John Wiley & Sons, Inc., 1976.
A Psychiatrist's World: The Selected Papers of Karl Menninger. New York: The Viking Press, 1959
Perls, F. S. *Ego, Hunger and Aggression: The Beginning of Gestalt Therapy.* New York: Vintage Press, 1969.
Rogers, Carl R. *On Becoming a Person: A Therapist's View of Psychotherapy.* Boston: Houghton Mifflin Co., 1961.
Rokeach, Milton. *The Nature of Human Values.* New York: The Free Press, 1973.

Sax, Saville, and Sandra Holleander. *Reality Games: Games People Ought to Play.* New York: Popular Library, 1972.

Schachtel, Ernest G. *Metamorphosis: New Light on the Conflict of Human Development and the Psychology of Creativity.* New York: Basic Books, Inc., 1959.

Schachter, Stanley. *The Psychology of Affiliation.* Stanford, Cal.: Stanford University Press, 1959.

Schutz, William. *Joy: Expanding Human Awareness.* New York: Grove Press, Inc., 1967.

Stahmann, Robert F., and Heibert, William J., eds., *Klemer's Counseling: Marital and Sexual Problems,* 2nd ed. Baltimore, Md.: The Williams and Wilkins Company, 1977.

Stein, Barry A. and Rosabeth Moss Kanter. "Building the Parallel Organization: Creating Mechanisms for Permanent Quality of Work Life". *The Journal of Applied Behavioral Science,* Vol. XVI, No. 3 (1980).

Twerski, Abraham J. *Like Yourself* *and Others Will Too.* Englewood Cliffs, N.J.: Prentice-Hall Publishing Co., Inc., 1978.

Veiga, J. F. "The Mobile Manager at Mid-Career". *Harvard Business Review,* Vol. LI (1973) 115-119.

Walton, Richard. *Interpersonal Peacemaking: Confrontations and Third Party Consulting.* Reading, Mass.: Addison-Wesley Publishing Co., Inc., 1969.

Watzlauick, Paul, Janet Helmick Beavin, and Don Jackson. *Pragmatics of Human Communication: A Study of Interactional Patterns, Pathologies and Paradoxes.* New York: W. W. Norton & Co., Inc., 1967.

Weaver, H. G. *The Mainspring of Human Progress.* New York: Foundation for Economic Education, Inc., 1953.

Whyte, William H., Jr. *The Organization Man.* Garden City, N.Y.: Doubleday, Anchor Books, 1956.

Zaleznik, Abraham, et al. *Orientation and Conflict in Career.* Boston: Harvard University Press, 1969.

Index

Achievement, 6, 79
Allocation, power use style, 32–33, 35, 57, 75, 95
 in large organizations, 35
 loss of influence in, 57
 overuse of style, 57
 nature of, 32–33

Belief systems, behavior in accord with, 6. *See also* Values conflict
Biofeedback, 124
Bureaucracies, 75, 76, 79. *See also* Organizations

Case study, of power and self-esteem, in corporation:
 acquisition, recent, description of, 100, 102
 communication failure, 108
 controller's organization, in main plant, 104
 decisions, influences on, 109
 description, 100
 economies, problems with, 102, 103
 employees, meetings with, 113
 and feedback to employees from general manager, 108–9
 improvement in performance, chart, 110
 objectives, setting of, 110, 111, 112
 operations, department, in main plant, 105–7
 organization chart, 101
 plan, summary of, 114
 problems with, 102, 103
 questions to ask self, 99–100, 113–14
 remote plant, problems and people in, 103–4
 sales and marketing, in main plant, 105–7
 strategic development plan, 110–13
 summary of problems, 107–8
 training, 111
 turnover, 105
 unresolved problems, 109
Charismatic power style:
 Goldwater, Barry, 58
 Johnson, Lyndon B., 58
 overuse, 57, 58
Citizen action groups, 14–15
 evolution of tactics, 14
 leaders in, 15
 as power blocs, 15
Conflict, and power, 63–67
 commonality of, 63, 64
 and lowered self-esteem, 65
 and power style overuse, 64, 65
 questions to ask self, 63
 steps to take, 66
 third party, use of to cure problems, 65–66

Diets, 124
 and stress, 124
Dilemmas, moral: *See* Values conflict
Divorce, 47

Effective communication, elements of, 19
Effectiveness, 58–59
 table, 58
Employees, problems of:
 discussion, 17
 loss of, self-esteem, 17
 older beliefs, 17
 unemployment, 17
Employees, self-esteem of, constraints on and approaches to increase of, 127–32
 alternative organization structure, 129–30
 empowerment of people, 127, 128
 making permanent, 128
 matrix structure, 129
 parallel organization, criteria to meet, 130–31
 problem-solving units, use, 132
 pyramid structure, 128
 quality circles, 130
 satisfaction with self vs. satisfaction with job, 127
 shadow structure in organizations, 128–29
Equifinality, concept of:
 example, 86
 mutual conditioning, 85
 nature, 85
 and organizations, 85, 86
Ethical questions, work with, 18–19. *See also* Values, conflict
 in business executives, 18
 case, 19
Executives: *See* Organization: *entries under* Power

Fear, of use of power, 25–28
 confrontation, 27, 28
 and early man, 25–26
 and extramarital relations, 27
 and giving away of power, 28
 and guilt, 27
 marriage, failure, of, 27
 modern complexity, 26
 nurture of, 26
 organization, problems in, 26
 solitude, fear of, 26–27
 and unemployment, 26
Feedback, 86–87
 in corporation, 87
 in human body, 86
 in thermostat, 87
Feedback, and self-esteem, 11–12
 lack, effects, 12
 organizational resistance, 12
Force, discussion, 24–25

Growth, 87–88
 in business organizations, 88
 individuals, 88
 learning, behavior of, 87
 in open systems, 87
 stepwise nature of, 87, 88
Guilt, 27

Includer style, of power use, 30–31, 35, 53–54
 aimlessness caused by overuse, 54
 overuse, 53, 54
Individuals, as systems:
 allocation style, 95
 authoritarian style, 91, 92
 and bureaucracies, 90
 early learning, 90
 employees, loss of self-esteem in, 92
 employees, rankings of in six companies, 93
 ethics, clash with, 94
 feedbacks, in organizations, 91
 functional groups, 92
 managers and supervisors, rankings of in six companies, 94
 metabolism, 89
 needs, meeting of, 90
 open vs. closed characteristics, 89–90
 and organizations, as closed systems, 90, 91, 92
 organizations, principles operating in, 91
 and powerlessness, revolts against, 97
 and rank of employee, 95
 total self-esteem, and employee rank, 96

Loss, and power, 67–68
 common experiences, 67
 effects, 68
 emotions, 68
 healing, 68
 and self-esteem sources, 67

Marriage, 27, 47
Maslow, Abraham, 77
Meditation, 124

Open systems, and power, 134
Organizations, nature of, and power:
  achievement motive, 79
  allocation style, 75
  and bureaucracy, 75, 76, 79
  causality, linear, 74
  and demand for power, 74
  dissatisfaction, 73
  and employees, needs of, 77, 78
  fakery, failure of, 79
  hierarchies, in Western view, 75
  mechanistic view of Universe, Western, 74–75
  modern attitudes to life, 80, 81
  and present U.S., 78
  self-esteem, needs for, 78, 79
  systems approach, 76, 77
  "underground" economy, 74
Others:
  power of, exercise about, 20–21
  value of self by, 6
Overuse of power styles, 54ff.

Personal power model, exercise in use of:
  Barkley, Scn. Albin, 35
  chart, 38
  Eisenhower, Gen. Dwight David, 35
  Johnson, Pres. Lyndon B., 35
  Lee, Gen. Robert E., 36
  Marshall, Gen. George, 35
  in organizations, 36
  overuse, 57, 58
  Patton, Gen. George, 35
  Rommel, Field Marshall Erwin, 37
  steps, 34
  styles, contrast of, 37
  styles, table, 34
  summary, 38–39
Physical activity, as stress control, 123
Planning, as self-esteem booster, 122
Power:
  defined, 25, 69, 70
  discussion, 1, 29–30, 33, 34, 133
  giving away of, 28, 55
  model, 30
  need for, 3–4
  and negative spiral, 3
  in open system, diagram, 134
  and personality, 2
  and positive spiral, 3
  recommendations, 135–36
  as stimulant, 45
  use, 29–30, 33, 34, 133, 135
Power styles, and self-esteem:
  assistant-to positions, power in, 46
  dilemmas, effects of, 50
  divorce, effects of, 47
  Duke of Medina Sidonia, 46
  Elizabeth I, Queen of England, 50
  entrepreneur, case, 44–45
  exploration, by children, 45
  feeding of self, in infancy, 44
  Hawkins, John, 50
  long term, 44
  managers, work with, 45
  Marquis of Santa Cruz, 46
  Napoleon Bonaparte, experience of in Italian campaigns, 48–49
  paired styles, 47, 48
  Philip II, King of Spain, 46
  power over others, use and style, 49
  power as stimulant, 45
  right vs. wrong in children, 45
  self-esteem sources, table, and power style, 51
  and self-set goals, 47–48
  sharing, effects of, 46–47
  short-term, 44
  and sources of self-esteem, 43
  Spanish Armada of 1588, 46
  Wynter, William, 50
  summary, 51
  young children, conditioning of, 44
Powerlessness:
  in conversation, 1
  and decreased self-esteem, 1
  in early life, 2
  revolts against, 97
Professional, power style, nature, 31, 36
Professional power style, overuse:
  as giveaway of power, 55
  loss of clarity of objective, 55, 56
  in technical organization, 56
Programs for stress control, commercial, 125

Rehearsal, as self-esteem booster, 122–23
Relaxation, 125

144 / Index

Rest, and stress, 123
Risk, general question of, 17–18
  author, experience of, 18

Self, power use summary about, questionnaire, 39, 40, 41
Self-esteem: *See also entries under Power*
  awareness of, 8
  building of against stress, 121–22
  and choice to be nonconfrontive, 20
  and deliberate choice to use power, 25
  and deliberate increase of, 8
  early, components and sources of, 9, 10
  elements of, 1, 2
  hydraulic model of, 7
  low, effects of, 7
  low, usual feelings of, 19–20
  loss of, effects of, 5ff.
  in open system, diagram, 134
  present, sources of, 9, 10
  process, 24
  and social activities, 122
  sources, 6ff.
  traumatic events, 8
Self-esteem, and personal power, exercise about, 59–62
  auto dealership, description of, 59, 60
  evaluation of personnel, 61
  owners, attitudes of, 61, 62
  questions to ask self, 62
  salesmen, requirements on, 60
Sleep, and stress, 122
Social contacts, and self-esteem 23–24, 122
Sociology of power, 69–72
  can-do factors, 70
  and congruence with value systems, 71
  free enterprise, beliefs about, 70
  at highest levels of organizations, 72
  individuals vs. groups, 69, 70
  limits, effects of, 70
  in modern corporations, 70
  power, nature of, 69, 70
  summary about, 72
  want-to-do factors, 70
  "we-ness," 71
Stress, and power, 115–21
  key to control, 120
  loneliness at top, 119
  and low self-esteem, 115
  mid-life crisis, 119–20
  physical adaptation, 116
  powerless action, 117
  questions to ask self, 117–18
  rigidity, onset of, 117
  roles, effects of, 118, 119
  senior levels, 119
  signs of on job, 120, 121
  stress cycle, 115–16, 117
  work environment, 118–19
Supporter, power style, 32, 54, 55
  nature, 32
  overuse, 54–55
  toadying, 55
  in White House, 54
Systems analysis:
  auto engine, 84
  battery, 84
  closed system, 83, 84
  living system, 83, 84
  mop in water, and entropy, 84
  open system, 83, 84
  people, 85

Therapy, for stress, 125

Values conflict:
  dilemma, 13
  effects, 12, 13
  and pollution, case, 12
  and power, use of, 14
  tactics to solve, 13, 14
Virtuoso, power use style:
  effects of overuse, 56
  Hitler, Adolf, case, 57
  nature, 31–32, 37

Will, to power, 25
Women:
  in business, 15
  expectations of, 15
  home, later emptiness of, 16
  loss of self-esteem by, 15, 16
  marriage, failure of, 16
  risks, 16, 17
  use of personal power by, 16, 17
Work, use of power at, choice of, 23
Worthiness, nature of, 25